THE CAPTIVE CONSCIENCE

The Captive Conscience

AN HISTORICAL PERSPECTIVE
OF THE CHRISTADELPHIAN STAND
AGAINST MILITARY SERVICE

John Botten

CHRISTADELPHIAN MILITARY SERVICE COMMITTEE
c/o THE CHRISTADELPHIAN
404 SHAFTMOOR LANE
BIRMINGHAM B28 8SZ, UK
2003

First published 2002
Reprinted 2003

ISBN 0 85189 151 9

©2003 Christadelphian Magazine & Publishing Association Ltd

Printed in England by
The Cromwell Press Limited
Trowbridge
Wiltshire

PREFACE

THIS book is written for a generation of believers who may have grown up with the impression that war was something that challenged disciples in the past, or might do so in the distant future. We are now realising that another time of testing could be upon us very soon—in some parts of the world it has already begun. We all therefore need to remember where we stand on matters of conscience in regard to war, and remind ourselves how brethren and sisters conducted themselves in earlier times of tribulation.

The world is changing—and with it the nature of warfare. If much of the 20th century was scarred by two world-wide conflicts involving large armies across many battle fronts, the last 20 years have seen different kinds of conflict marked by fervid nationalism, brutal acts of atrocity against rival groups and an increased disregard for any so called 'rules of war' or conscientious objection.

The world has also become less sympathetic to believers. Crises blow up very quickly in this age of instantaneous communications. Many of the wars since 1945 around the world have been 'civil' wars and they have been marked by a blurring of the distinction between civilians and the military. Tolerance of minority viewpoints has diminished in many countries. Prophecy suggests that things will get worse before the coming of the Lord Jesus Christ and that the faith of believers will be tested greatly. This makes the message all the more urgent today.

One feature of the book is the frequent use of anecdotal evidence. Some of this is typical of the experience of brethren and sisters, many of whom experienced relatively little difficulty in gaining exemption. Other extracts are included because they illustrate extremes of suffering resulting from a brother's or sister's objection to military service. As such they are exceptional, but they do illustrate that some faced suffering, imprisonment and even death for their faith. I would like to thank all those who sent accounts of these experiences, even though they represent but a small portion of the total experience of our community.

This illustrative material has been included because the work is not about an anonymous body of people, but about individual brethren and sisters and how they reacted to the challenge of upholding the Truth in difficult times. Conscientious objection is an individual responsibility, as well as one which we all share as an element of our fellowship in Christ. Discipleship, like history, is about people; and that is its true challenge.

Solihull   JOHN BOTTEN

ACKNOWLEDGEMENTS

THIS book would not have been possible but for the willing contributions of many brethren and sisters who lived through some of the events it recounts, particularly those related to the Second World War. It owes much, too, to brethren from other countries who provided material, checked first drafts and provided much evidence of the worldwide nature of our fellowship. Particular mention needs to be made of the Military Service Committee of the United Kingdom, who first proposed a booklet on the subject—and got rather more than they anticipated.

JCB

> Illustrations have been included from non-copyright sources. Circulars, forms, certificates etc. are reproduced from material supplied to the author or in the archives of the Christadelphian Office.

FOREWORD

ABOUT the time of the Gulf War (1990-1991), the UK Military Service Committee was brought up against the realisation that the crisis might not be ended, nor its scope contained, as quickly and as narrowly as proved to be the case. There was always the possibility that a "great matter" might be the outcome of the relatively "little fire" which Saddam Hussein had kindled: and it was 45 years since the end of the Second World War. With the exception of the Falklands Crisis (1982), little had happened to alert the Brotherhood to the possibility that it might again need to state its case to the authorities, and once more seek exemption from military service: the word "conscription" might be heard again. The Military Service Committee received anxious enquiries and concern was expressed that our stand on matters of conscientious objection should be refreshed and updated.

It was felt, therefore, that a refresher course would not come amiss, to keep bright the armour of the soldiers of the gospel of peace. Brother John Botten, a trained historian, was therefore asked to produce an historical perspective on the attitude of the Brotherhood to military service. *The Captive Conscience* is the outcome. It draws attention to obligations to the precepts of the Lord Jesus which must not be sidestepped, and reminds us of matters which may yet severely test our consciences before Christ returns.

The work is Brother John Botten's own, but the members of the Military Service Committee felt themselves involved in what he has written and now commend to the Christadelphian Brotherhood worldwide these reflections on a vital element of the faith which we hold as disciples of Christ.

North Cave   ALFRED NORRIS

CONTENTS

PREFACE v
ACKNOWLEDGEMENTS vi
FOREWORD vii
1. A HOUSE UNITED 1
2. THE ROMAN WORLD 9
3. THE MIDDLE AGES AND AFTER 15
4. THE PROTESTANT CENTURIES 18
5. FROM CIVIL WAR TO WORLD WAR 23
6. "YOUR KING AND COUNTRY NEED YOU!" 29
7. BETWEEN THE WARS 52
8. CONSCIENTIOUS OBJECTION IN THE SECOND WORLD WAR 54
9. CONSCIENTIOUS OBJECTION AFTER THE SECOND WORLD WAR 80
10. CHRISTADELPHIAN CONSCIENTIOUS OBJECTORS IN OTHER LANDS 84
11. CONCLUSIONS 113
BIBLIOGRAPHY 123
INDEX 129

THE CAPTIVE CONSCIENCE

> *"You have heard that it was said, 'An eye for an eye and a tooth for a tooth.' But I tell you not to resist an evil person ... Love your enemies ... and pray for those who spitefully use you and persecute you, that you may be sons of your Father ..."*
> THE WORDS OF JESUS IN MATTHEW 5:38,39,44,45

> *"If it is possible, as much as depends on you, live peaceably with all men. Beloved, do not avenge yourselves, but rather give place to wrath ... Do not be overcome by evil, but overcome evil with good."*
> THE APOSTLE PAUL IN ROMANS 12:18,19,21

> *"But Peter and the other apostles answered and said: 'We ought to obey God rather than men.'"*
> ACTS 5:29

EXCEPT WHERE SHOWN, ALL QUOTATIONS FROM THE BIBLE ARE FROM THE NEW KING JAMES VERSION

1
A HOUSE UNITED

THE year: 1864. The place: the United States of America. The circumstances: a bitter civil war begun in 1861, a war which in the end would cost the lives of 620,000 men and bring to a head the issue of conscription for those trying to follow the commandments of Christ.

At the time there was no Christadelphian community, or at least not one known by that name. A doctor called John Thomas had established small groups of those who shared his belief in the gospel as it had been taught by the apostles. These groups in the United States and Britain called themselves by a variety of names, although they commonly referred to those who shared their faith and baptism as "brothers and sisters". These small groups were found in both Northern and Southern States and so now found themselves divided by the conflict and isolated from each other, although Brother Thomas continued to visit wherever he could, crossing from one side to another to strengthen the new ecclesias.

Even before the outbreak of fighting, brethren had written to *The Herald of the Kingdom and Age to Come*, the Bible magazine produced by Brother Thomas, to ask what they should do in the event of war. The answer was forthright:

> "Our conviction is that Christians should leave the devil to fight his own battles; and that if he sought to compel them to serve in his ranks, they ought to refuse to do so ... Let the potsherds of the earth strive together and Christians stand aloof."
>
> (Reply to a letter, March 1860)

In the event of compulsion, there would be no shame in fleeing to a place of safety; if imprisoned, they were to bear their loss of liberty rather than fight. As Brother Thomas wrote on another occasion, if the members of other churches of the day chose to fight against each other, "let them do it to their hearts' content, but let not Christians mingle in the unhallowed strife."

Thus, right from the start of the Christadelphian community, a clear stand was made against military service.[1]

Exemption on Religious Grounds

At first there was no shortage of volunteers anxious to do their bit for their part of the country, seeking excitement, ashamed to stay at home when others had gone to serve, or lured into volunteering by bounty payments. Nonetheless, by 1862, a series of setbacks, and the fear that those who had enlisted at the start of the War would leave as soon as the year for which they had enlisted was up, led the

Fighting in the American Civil War

Southern States to bring in conscription of all young men between the ages of 18 and 35. Those enrolled were allowed 30 days to volunteer, and were then supposed to join the Confederate Army. In fact, the draft, as it became known, was deeply unpopular, and exemptions were many and varied. Apart from exemption on medical grounds, those drafted could also hire a substitute to go for them, or pay $500. The law also allowed for exemption on religious grounds, although those baptized after the passing of the law had no right of exemption and, late in the War, a motion to expel all conscientious objectors from the South was brought before the Confederate Congress, only to be defeated.

A HOUSE UNITED

Volunteering went so well in the North at first that recruiting was suspended in April 1862. However, a series of setbacks for the North led to a call for 300,000 volunteers, and the Militia Law of July 1862 made it compulsory for all 18-45 year olds to register. As in the South, this was a very unpopular law and evasion was widespread. Here, too, men simply disappeared into the forests, paid a $300 fine, found a substitute, or served in hospitals. Only 7% of those drafted actually served.

As it turned out, the threat of the early brethren being forced to fight was not great, but they were not to know that at the time.

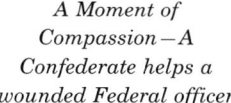

A Moment of Compassion — A Confederate helps a wounded Federal officer

The First Petition

Right from the start, the brethren sought to make their position clear. In the South, a petition was submitted as early as 1862 to the Confederate government by a group of brethren acting under the name of "The Nazarenes"[2]. Their claim was:

> "Christ is our lawgiver, master, king, and, as 'no man can serve two masters', and we have chosen His service, therefore we owe undivided and perfect allegiance to Him. We cannot and do not owe allegiance to any other …"

> "… the philosophy of this age is not the Christian's rule or law … (and) institutions of human origin are … at enmity with God … We could not … conscientiously be found actively engaged in co-operation with 'the powers that be' to sustain them in their proposed designs; for we believe that the present visitations are of God …"

Reproduced in The Christadelphian, 1940, page 411

THE CAPTIVE CONSCIENCE

However, sometimes more immediate methods were needed to counter the threat of conscription. Brethren in Henderson City, in the Southern State of Kentucky, came to Brother Thomas with their concern about conscription, and he decided to take advantage of the exemption allowed to ministers of religion. Accordingly, he arranged for certificates to be prepared for a total of ten brethren stating "that - - - is a Minister of the Gospel and conscientiously opposed to bearing arms". Although this is not a practical solution for every occasion, Brother Thomas' instinctive thinking in Kentucky illustrated his conviction that each disciple is, truly, a minister of Christ who stands before worldly authorities as an individual, and not just as a member of a group.

The Name "Christadelphian"

In the North, the Law gave exemption to those "who belonged to a denomination conscientiously opposed to the bearing of arms". The brethren there were just as determined to follow their Lord.

> "The brethren of Ogle County," wrote Brother Thomas, "have a mortal distaste for all ... compromise ... Their determination is to be shot at their doors, rather than serve in the armies of the North and South."

Since he was passing through that part of Illinois, Brother Thomas was asked to put something in writing for these brethren to present to the court. In order to file their petition, the brethren needed their religious community to be named. Brother Thomas pondered the requirement and came up with the name "Christadelphian", based on the two Greek words *Christou adelphoi* (meaning 'Brethren of or in Christ')[3] and incorporated this name in the following certificate:

> "This is to certify that - - - - - - and others, constitute a religious association, denominated herein for the sake of distinguishing them from all other 'Names and Denominations', *Brethren in Christ*, or in one word, *Christadelphians*; and that said brethren are in fellowship with similar associations in England, Scotland, the British Provinces, New York, and other cities of the North and South—New York being for the time present the radiating centre of their testimony to the people of the current age and generation of the world.

This is also to certify, that the denomination constituted of the associations or ecclesias of this Name, conscientiously opposes, and earnestly protests against 'Brethren in Christ' having anything to do with politics in wordy strife, or arms-bearing in the service of the Sin-powers of the world under any conceivable circumstances or conditions whatever; regarding it as a course of conduct disloyal to the Deity in Christ, their Lord and King, and perilous to their eternal welfare!

This being individually and collectively the conscientious conviction of all true Christadelphians, they claim and demand the rights and privileges so considerately accorded by the Congress of the United States, in the statute made and provided for the exemption of members of a denomination conscientiously opposed to bearing arms in the service of any human government.

*Title page of the pamphlet **Yahweh Elohim**, referred to below*

יְהוָה אֱלֹהִים
YAHWEH ELOHIM;
OR,
A TESTIMONY
IN BEHALF OF
Original Apostolic Christianity.
REVIVED IN THE
NINETEENTH CENTURY
IN
BRITAIN AND AMERICA.

This is also further to certify that the undersigned is the personal instrumentality by which the Christian Association aforesaid in Britain and America has been developed within the last fifteen years, and that, therefore, he knows assuredly that a conscientious, determined, and uncompromising opposition to serving in the armies of the 'powers that be' is their denominational characteristic. In confirmation of this, he appeals to the definition of its position in respect of war, on page 13 of a pamphlet entitled *Yahweh Elohim*, issued by the Antipas Association of Christadelphians assembling at 24 Cooper Institute, New York, and with which he ordinarily convenes. Advocates of war and desolation are not in fellowship with them or with the undersigned.—JOHN THOMAS"

THE CAPTIVE CONSCIENCE

And so it was that, at the County Courthouse in Oregon, Illinois, the name "Christadelphian" was first publicly used in connection with the obtaining of exemption from military service. "I did not know a better denomination ... this declares their true status", Brother Thomas wrote.

A Petition to Congress

The certificate was satisfactory for the brethren in Ogle County, but John Thomas went on, in March 1865, to draft a petition addressed to the US Congress, designed to provide for the wider community. The text of the petition was reproduced in *The Ambassador* for May 1865, pages 169/170. In fact, because the Civil War came to an end and conscription laws were suspended, the petition was never presented, but it provided a model for the future.

In 1864, then, the community which had variously been called The Royal Association of Believers, The Antipas Association, Nazarenes, or even Thomasites[4], now had a name. Those who have seen the name Christadelphian mangled or misspelled may well feel that the simple title "Brethren in Christ" would have served as well. But we should surely be content that the name of our community—one that marks us out clearly from so many other Christian denominations—arose at a time and in circumstances when such a stand was being made.

Every time we use the name Christadelphian we should remember that it was first used publicly to uphold the commandments of the Master in the midst of a bitter Civil War.

Hardship

Little evidence remains of the hardships which some of our brethren went through, but circumstances of this period are detailed by Brother Thomas in a letter dated February 1865, part of which is reproduced opposite.

Thus in the midst of a War which divided their fellows and might have brought brother face to face with brother in combat, our early brethren remained united in their determination to take a stand for what they knew was right.

... You may perhaps like to hear how our brethren have been getting along in the Confederate States during the past three years. In Richmond and Lunenburg County, Virginia, they are all well and prosperous. A son of one of them who has been three years in the army of the South, is a prisoner on parole, and residing with me till he can get something to do. Believing it is wrong to be killing men, he put himself in a position to be captured. His captors sent him on North, and as I said, he is now with me. All I know of the brethren is from him. They hold their meetings regularly, and take no part in the war. The Confederate Congress passed an act, exempting them from military service, under the name of Nazarenes, on payment of 500 dollars. All are exempted who were members at the time of passing the act; but all who join them since, are liable to military conscription. My informant has four brothers in the army. One obeyed the gospel recently. He applied for his discharge, stating that he could not conscientiously use his weapons to destroy life. But his superiors reviled him. He appealed to his past service in twelve of the bloodiest battles of the war; and to his reputation with his comrades, in proof that it was not cowardice that caused his application. His valour was admitted, but conscience was ignored. He has often charged the enemy with his troop, but he will not kill. This course has arrested the notice of his captain, who has come to recognize the existence of conscience formed by the truth. On one occasion, he went into a charge in which all his company were killed or wounded except himself. His Captain said it was suicide, and he determined that he should expose himself no more. He was put therefore in a position in which he would not be called upon to fight. None of the brethren have lost any of their sons. How it may be if the war continues, who can tell? There was a motion made in the Confederate Congress, to drive them all out of the country! Had this been decreed, I should have despaired of Richmond and the South. But "the Earth helped the Woman." An able speech was made on their defence, and the motion was lost ...

Ambassador of the Coming Age, April 1865, page 158

---

1. It is worth noting that John Thomas had consistently opposed Christian involvement in war. As early as 1835 he wrote in *The Apostolic Advocate* that the church was not "to locate themselves amid the din of arms, the clangour of trumpets and the roll of the drums". Again, in 1849, after completing *Elpis Israel*, Brother Thomas attended a meeting of the "Peace Society" in London: when he eventually rose to make his contribution to the debate, he said, "... that national

THE CAPTIVE CONSCIENCE

wars to avenge the injured, and defend liberty, are neither impious nor impolitic, (and) that while *a Bible Christian must not fight* in the absence of the captain of his salvation, the Scriptures leave the nations to do as they please, holding them, however, NATIONALLY RESPONSIBLE for the *principles and manner* in which they make war" (*Dr. Thomas: His Life and Work*, page 179).

2. John Thomas wrote in *The Ambassador* (1868, page 315): "During the war, the brethren [in Virginia] called themselves Nazarenes [sometimes spelled Nazarines], under which name they obtained exemption from military service." This exemption was granted to brethren in the South as a result of a petition submitted by the Nazarene brethren as early as 1862. The full text was reproduced in *The Christadelphian* in 1940 (page 411) and the circumstances have been further researched by Brother Peter Hemingray, to be published under the title *Dr. Thomas: His Faith and His Friends*. Other information has been gleaned by Michael Casey: see Bibliography.

3. Although this is the literal translation of *Christou adelphoi*, the less accurate translation "Brethren *in* Christ" has often been preferred and was used by Brother Thomas himself in his diary account of the origin of the name. In the New Testament, none of the early apostles presumed to call themselves "Brethren of Christ", although on a number of occasions, the Lord Jesus called his disciples his brethren. The Lord may deign to call us brother (or sister), but we must bow to him and call him Lord. Even James, the Lord's natural brother, calls himself only "a bondservant of Jesus Christ" in James 1:1. But we are members of God's family in Christ and hence brothers and sisters of one another *in* him.

4. In a letter which can be seen at the Christadelphian Office, Brother Thomas writes: "The reason why I have got the brethren to adopt the name Christadelphian is to save them from being called Thomasites."

2

CONSCIENTIOUS OBJECTORS IN THE ROMAN WORLD

THE stand taken by the brethren of 1864 was not a new one. Right from the time of the apostles the early Christians had been taught that they should not use force against their enemies, no matter the degree of provocation.

Those 1st Century believers who first heard the Gospel of Jesus Christ or listened to the reading of the letters written by the apostles could be in no doubt as to the teaching of their Lord. It is remarkable that any unbiased reader should misinterpret the clear words of Scripture:

"You have heard that it was said, 'An eye for an eye and a tooth for a tooth'. But I tell you not to resist an evil person. But whoever slaps you on your right cheek, turn the other to him also ... You have heard that it was said, 'You shall love your neighbour and hate your enemy'. But I say to you, love your enemies ... pray for those who ... persecute you, that you may be sons of your Father in heaven."

(Matthew 5:38,39,43-45)

These words of Jesus were echoed in equally clear words from the Apostle Paul, writing to believers in Rome, the military centre of his day:

"Repay no one evil for evil ... live peaceably with all men. Beloved, do not avenge yourselves, but rather give place to wrath; for it is written, 'Vengeance is mine, I will repay,' says the Lord. Therefore if your enemy is hungry, feed him; if he is thirsty, give him a drink ... Do not be overcome by evil, but overcome evil with good." (Romans 12:17-21)

Consequently it is not surprising to find that the question of taking part in military service was not regarded as an issue worthy of further debate; the commandment of Christ was clear and unequivocal: military service was not for brethren in Christ. It is therefore natural that Josephus makes no mention of Christians joining in the violence which preceded and followed the Jewish revolt of AD 70, although there is reference to Christians trapped in Jerusalem fleeing from the city during the unexpected lull in the siege foreseen by the Lord 40 years earlier.

However, one consequence of the Jewish revolt was a sharper than ever divide between Jewish nationalists, who fought to the death against the Romans, and their fellow Jews who had become Christians and not only refused to fight, but also rightly saw in the Roman advance on Jerusalem a tragic fulfilment of the prophecies uttered by Jesus.

Roman Victory Procession

Apart from this very real hostility to Jewish Christians there was little threat to the faith of most early brethren. The teaching of Jesus was very clear and the idolatrous associations of Roman military ceremonies made it even less likely that young brethren should wish to join the legions, whilst Jews, and therefore Jewish Christians, were exempt from military service. Conscription was rarely enforced except in newly conquered territories. Except for those who were baptized whilst serving in the army, there seems to have been little difficulty, and concerning converts from the army, such as Cornelius, we have no Scriptural evidence on which conclusions can be based. How long the early Christians maintained their stand is hard to detect, but by late in the 2nd Century there are references to "Christians" in the Roman army.[1] The pressure to conform, and the temptations of army life, became all too persuasive as the drift away from the original gospel accelerated.

Nonetheless, Roman writers of the time reflect the issues being debated in the Church of the 2nd and 3rd centuries. Often their views appear to face both ways. Tertullian, writing at the very end of the 2nd Century, decried killing and destruction, but said that war was necessary, and talked about praying "for brave armies". He also argued that Christians were loyal citizens, and claimed that Christians were found in every military camp; at the same time as saying that it is "better to be slain than to slay". A few years later he seems less equivocal:

> "How will a Christian man go to war? Indeed, how will he serve even in peacetime without a sword which the Lord has taken away?"—Tertullian, *Treatise on Idolatry*, AD 211

Emperor Worship

The major issues for Tertullian were loyalty and idolatry; loyalty to the Emperor within the framework of loyalty to God, and idolatry because of the religious significance of much of Roman army practice. This was particularly marked in the worship of the Roman standards and in the *sacramentum*, a sacred oath to the Emperor recited twice each year. The army camp also has been described by one writer as "a portable sacred city".

Other Christian writers of the same period still reflect the apostles' teaching on the use of force. Hippolytus includes serving as gladiators in his list of occupations forbidden to Christians and advises that a baptized Christian wanting to become a soldier should be disfellowshipped. Origen is equally clear:

> "Jesus considered it contrary to his divinely inspired legislation to approve any kind of homicide whatsoever ... we no longer take up the sword against any nation, nor do we learn the art of war any more."—Origen, *Against Celsus*

Yet, at the same time, Origen laid one of the foundation stones of the arguments later put forward in favour of fight-

THE CAPTIVE CONSCIENCE

ing in a "just war" by suggesting that Christians should "pray to God on behalf of those who are fighting a righteous cause". In compromising his neutrality towards the world's warfare, Origen was taking a step towards accepting the necessity of fighting which would afterwards undermine the principle of refusing military service.

Despite Origen's words, Christians continue to appear in accounts of army life, not least in the story told by Eusebius in the late 3rd Century about the "Thundering Legion", the name given to the 12th Legion after it had been delivered from disaster on the Danube frontier by thunder and lightning allegedly brought on by the prayers of Christian soldiers.

By the time of Augustine at the end of the 4th Century, the struggle to maintain the commandments of Christ by standing out against the use of force had been lost. In his book *The City of God*, this highly influential bishop from North Africa argued that war was justified to resist the barbarians, who threatened both the empire and the church. The church must pray for the defeat of evil by the Emperor—for victory would be a sign of Divine favour and the justice of the cause being defended.

Coin of the Emperor Diocletian AD 284-305

In all this, some remained true to their faith. From the time of the Emperor Diocletian at the end of the 3rd Century, there were a number of accounts of Christians executed for refusing to join in idolatrous practices associated with the army. But the most notable example concerns a young man called Maximilian, who in AD 295 was just 21. By this time it was becoming harder to recruit volunteers, and since Maximilian was a fit young man he was brought before the local Roman governor. He steadfastly refused to serve in the Army, saying that he was a Christian and could only serve Christ. Asked why he would not join other Christians in the Army, he replied: "They know what is fitting for them; but I am a Christian and I cannot do evil." Maximilian was put to death for his refusal to serve. Ironically, the very church which had taken the view that warfare was justifiable, afterwards canonised Maximilian for his stand against fighting.

What can we learn from these early centuries?

Firstly, it is astonishing how quickly men can turn to "another gospel". The teaching of the first disciples of the Lord was very clear: they were not to fight or resist evil. Yet, within a few generations, reasons were found for soldiers to continue in the Roman Army, and by the 4th Century Augustine had justified war as the positive duty of the Christian in defence of a "just" Roman cause. Once the Empire became officially Christian, the Roman Catholic Church became totally committed to supporting the Roman Army, and has remained willing to support warfare in a "just cause" ever since.

Secondly, it is worth noting that this change came about because Christians wanted the Romans to defeat the heathen barbarians, fearing what would otherwise happen to them. As a result, their loyalties became divided, and it became harder to resist the argument for fighting. After all, if Christians were willing to pray for a Roman victory and to rejoice when the barbarians were defeated, would they not be a little hypocritical then to refuse to fight?

This also represents a considerable challenge to us. It is all too easy to get drawn into expressions of support for military or police successes against those who commit atrocities in peace or war. We need to remember that such comments by conscientious objectors can easily attract accusations of hypocrisy and be very cautious in what we say.

It is clearly inconsistent for the disciple of Christ to applaud military action by any power or party and then to refuse to fight. This inconsistency weakened and eventually broke the resolve of the church in Roman times to follow faithfully the commandments of Christ regarding violence. Increasingly the church began to justify warfare, forgetting all too easily the teaching and practices of the Lord Jesus Christ and the earliest disciples.[2]

---

1. The word Christian has been used throughout as a general term for those who professed to follow Christ, without regard as to whether they faithfully followed his teaching as set out in the New Testament.

2. Fuller details of the Roman period are given in *The Christian and War* by Brother J. B. Norris, pages 15-29.

3

THE MIDDLE AGES AND AFTER

AFTER the collapse of the Roman Empire, there is little evidence about minority religious beliefs. As a result it is difficult to estimate how many kept alive the faith which had been taught by the apostles. However, the mediæval chronicles do tell us quite a lot about the attitude to military service of the Catholic Church, which dominated Europe during this period.

At first, warfare in the Middle Ages was conducted on foot by a warrior class, with little mobilisation of the general populace; although, when raiders such as the Vikings attacked Britain, every fit man might be expected to help resist them. Later on, with the advent of the mounted knight, warfare became the occupation of an aristocratic elite. Although some peasants on a mediæval estate might be expected to accompany their lord to battle, most would stay at home tilling the lord's lands.

The tendency to turn warfare into a Christian duty accelerated during much of the Middle Ages. Although popes and bishops might decry the excesses of local wars between rival barons, and call for truces such as the "Peace of God",[1] their words were often contradictory. There was a widespread feeling that killing non-Christians was noble, as the famous Charlemagne, who later became Holy Roman Emperor, wrote to the Pope in 796:

> "Our task is to defend the holy Church of Christ with arms against the attack of pagans and devastation by infidels from without ... Your task, most holy father, is to lift up your hands to God, like Moses, so as to aid our troops ..."

When the Christian armies of Charlemagne faced the invading Moslems in Spain, the *Chanson de Roland* tells how the soldiers were told by Archbishop Turpin:

THE CAPTIVE CONSCIENCE

"If you should chance to die today, then you will be holy martyrs and will win a place in Paradise ..."

Knighthood became associated with elaborate rituals. By the 12th Century, the young knight-to-be was bathed in 'holy' water, and dressed in a pure white tunic; and was required to pray all through the night, his weapons placed before the altar. In the morning he would hear Mass and make his confession; and the priest would then dedicate the young man's sword in the name of the Trinity.

The Crusades—'Holy' War

The Crusades gave the ultimate expression to this raising of warfare to a religious duty. During more than two centuries, armies set out for the Near East invoking the name of Christ, whilst perpetrating the most appalling massacres of Jews and others on the way to Jerusalem. The Crusades, fought to free the holy city, became the ultimate expression of the argument for a holy war, and resulted in some of the worst atrocities committed in the name of Christianity.

Crusaders on their Way to the Holy Land

Whether there were any able to keep the light of the gospel burning through these long centuries is difficult to judge, especially as regards opposition to military service. There were so-called heretics tried by Catholic Church

THE MIDDLE AGES

courts and punished, some having crusades launched against them by the Catholic kings and lords of Europe. Trial evidence gives some glimpses of those who resisted the Catholic Church, but it is primarily evidence of the prosecution which remains, and this is often limited.

Some small non-conformist religious movements of the 12th and 13th Centuries are known to have professed religious pacifism. This later appeared in other small groups, including the followers of John Wycliffe in England, but the evidence concerning these groups is very limited.

One group which seems to have sought to maintain something of the apostles' faith was the "Vaudois" or "Waldensians". These groups of mediæval believers seem to have held a number of beliefs which we would recognise as Scriptural. Because the Catholic Church regarded such views as heresy, they were persecuted relentlessly in the 13th and 14th Centuries. Whilst there is little evidence of their views on warfare, they seem not to have resisted their persecutors by force, as some other groups opposed to the Catholic Church did, except in the later stages of persecution in the 15th Century and after. It is not until the Reformation that we find clear evidence of conscientious objection to fighting as a distinctive Bible-based belief.

---

1. The first "Peace of God" was proclaimed in Southern France in 989, and bound local nobles by an oath not to attack the poor, women and unarmed clergy. Later, under the "Truce of God", warfare was forbidden on certain holy days and during Lent.

4

THE PROTESTANT CENTURIES

"My conscience is captive to the Word of God ... Here I stand, I can do no other."

THESE words of Martin Luther sum up the stand which all those seeking to follow the Lord Jesus must take. Unfortunately, Luther's words were not always matched by his deeds. Although he took a stand against the corruption of the Mediæval Church, Luther continued to accept much traditional Catholic teaching. In particular, faced with the Peasants' War in which peasants, excited by the upheaval which the Reformation was bringing, began to attack their lords, he wrote an outspoken pamphlet *Against the Murdering, Thieving Hordes of the Peasants*. This justified the use of force to put down rebellion against the civil government, and marked the stage at which the Protestant movement became associated with the ruling classes in Germany. This association would lead with dreadful inevitability to the Thirty Years' War of 1618-48, fought largely in the name of religion but for very worldly motives, and to countless other acts of savagery carried out in the name of Christ.

Nonetheless, there were others who, having gone back to the Bible as the source of their faith, found that they could not in all conscience lift up their swords against their fellows, even though harried and persecuted themselves. Helped by the invention of movable type by Johann Gutenberg, and driven by the desire to preach the Scriptures to others, these groups used the printed word to spread their faith. As a result there is much evidence of the beliefs and practices of these scattered groups of men and women, who often had to meet in secret from fear of persecution, or whose livelihood was imperilled because their beliefs were considered to be dangerously unorthodox.

One such was Conrad Grebel, a student from Zürich, who became one of the leading figures amongst these "Brethren in Christ", as they called themselves. He was horrified at the excesses urged by Thomas Müntzer, the most notorious of the radical Protestant leaders of the peasants in Germany. In September 1524, shortly after the Peasants' War between radical Protestants and their rulers had begun, Grebel wrote as follows:

> "The gospel and its adherents are not to be protected by the sword, nor are they thus to protect themselves ... True Christian believers are sheep amongst wolves, sheep for the slaughter; they must be baptized in anguish and affliction, tribulation, persecution, suffering and death." Letter to Thomas Müntzer

Although Grebel escaped execution by his persecutors by dying of the Plague in 1526, his father was beheaded for his faith, suffering as his son had foreseen, and as many others of the Brethren would. That same year Michael Sattler, formerly a prior in a Catholic monastery, wrote:

> "Christians are quite at rest and confident in their Father in heaven, without any external worldly armour ... Christians are citizens of heaven, not of the world ... Men of this world are armed with iron, but the Christian is armed with the armour of God, that is with truth, justice, faith and the Word of God."

Michael Sattler was arrested in 1527 and put on trial by the Austrian authorities. One of the charges against him was that he would refuse to fight if the Turks invaded "Christian" lands. Like so many others of his day he was tortured and burned at the stake.

Admiration for Objectors

Many of those with whom these Brethren in Christ mixed were astonished at their attitudes, which included refusal of civil offices, involvement with police, and any occupation where it was necessary to use force. One Swiss writer commented:

> "They carry no weapon, neither sword nor dagger ... saying that these are wolf's clothing which should not be found on the sheep."

Most of the Brethren maintained their refusal to use force in the face of the utmost provocation. Even their enemies found it hard not to admire their way of life. As one Protestant commented:

> "Their walk and manner of life is altogether pious, holy and irreproachable."

The Stand of Polish Brethren

Nearly a century later, when some of the Brethren had taken refuge in Poland, the question of military service again came to the fore. The independence of Poland has always been fragile, and now the country was threatened by Turks and Tartars from the East and by its neighbours on all sides. Patriotic calls to arms were hard to resist, but Johann Wolzogen, an Austrian baron who became a humble preacher, set out the case for refusing military service, and even non-combatant service in the army:

> "A Christian has no homeland in this world. Therefore the little piece of this earth on which we were born is not worth risking either one's life or that of another ...
>
> Murder, even of an attacker, is still murder. Indeed there is a sort of hidden vengeance in it which is worse because it is carried out before the attacker has managed actually to commit the sin. If we let ourselves be killed by an enemy, it is not because we love him directly, but because it is for us to show Christian patience ...
>
> If a believer refuses to go around armed, God will surely not forsake him. Far more people have perished in the world when armed than when unarmed."

Interestingly enough his advice to hard-pressed believers follows the same line taken by Brother John Thomas:

> "In time of war, act like the sojourners we are, withdrawing little by little to places of safety (or) ... to another country ... To the faithful, God indicates flight or some other way of escape."

There is also an indication that even non-combatant service such as bringing up supplies, or acting as secretary to a general, was regarded as against the commandments of Christ and led to disfellowship of the offender.

> "The praiseworthy custom of debarring such for a time from the Lord's Table should be adopted."
>
> Johann Wolzogen writing in 1636

Elsewhere in Europe, other Bible-believers were coming to the same conclusions. John Biddle, a headteacher from Gloucestershire, published a statement of his faith in 1654 under the title *The Twofold Catechism*. This set out to give straightforward Bible answers to questions of faith. One section specifically covered the question of taking up the sword, echoing the stand of the Brethren against military service during the English Civil War, fought in part in the name of religion. Another statement of the time says:

> "The saints expect it as their portion patiently to suffer from the world, as the Scriptures direct them, than otherwise to attain the rule or government thereof."

Backdrop to the 19th Century

Of the 18th Century, so far little evidence has come to light of the activities of Brethren in Christ. The opposition of the established churches continued, although rarely in such fierce manner as in the 16th and 17th Centuries. The changing patterns of warfare also seem to have made the use of conscription less common. Nonetheless it is evident that the stand taken by Brother John Thomas in 1864 was founded on a long tradition of faithfulness to the Scriptures which had survived from the time of the Reformation onwards.

What can we learn from these Protestant centuries? Two things are strikingly clear.

The first is the faith of the Brethren in Christ who were willing to give their lives for the sake of the gospel and the Lord whom they loved. There is a quality of heroism to be found in these persecuted brethren and sisters which makes the quality of our lives in Christ in this comfortable 21st Century seem shallow. How would we fare in such persecution? Are we prepared to lay down our lives for the Master we serve?

The second is the consistency of their stand. "*My kingdom is not of this world*," said Jesus, and this was a central plank of their stand on conscientious objection. The other-worldliness of these believers is an example which we would do well to follow, in an age where pressures to conform are so strong. There has never been a time when it has been more important that our consciences should be captive to the word of the gospel.

5

FROM CIVIL WAR TO WORLD WAR

WE have already seen, in Chapter 1, how the American Civil War led to the Christadelphian community emerging as a distinct group conscientiously opposed to military service. The stand taken by the American brethren of that time, put into words by Brother Thomas, was utterly consistent with the Lord's teaching, and with the practices of those who had tried to follow that teaching in the intervening centuries.

Brother Thomas survived the Civil War, continuing his work for the Truth until his death in 1871. During the last years of his life he was associated closely with Brother Robert Roberts, a remarkable brother who helped to shape the life of the community through his tireless work. In 1864 he had founded the *Ambassador of the Coming Age*, which was renamed *The Christadelphian* in 1869. As its editor until his death in 1898, Robert Roberts helped form the ecclesial structure we know today, and had a continuing influence over the question of conscientious objection.

Robert Roberts' views on military service were consistent with those we have seen elsewhere. In 1868 he wrote:

"It is impossible that a Christadelphian can be a patriot or a soldier." *Ambassador of the Coming Age*, 1868, page 308

and in 1872:

"If we must pay heavy penalties, unless we choose to break the law of God, let the penalties be paid. If we must be killed and all our families with us, unless we forfeit the approbation of our Lord and Master ... let us die at once. We are not to consider consequences at all." *The Christadelphian*, 1872, page 489

That such a sacrifice might be necessary seemed quite possible in the latter half of the 19th Century, as European armies employed ever larger forces to try to overwhelm the

THE CAPTIVE CONSCIENCE

growing effectiveness of defenders. This was particularly the case when the advent of the machine gun rendered war on horseback suicidal, and enabled a handful of men, well dug in, to resist attack by a far larger number.

Millions under Arms

Conscription had been first used in modern Europe at the time of the French Revolution and the Napoleonic Wars. Both France and Prussia had relied on conscripted men to some extent, but in island Britain the power of the Navy, and a long-standing suspicion of large standing armies as a threat to liberty, meant that recruitment was voluntary, in theory at least: in practice, unsuspecting young men who had drunk too much might wake up to find that they had been press-ganged into the Navy, or having inadvertently "taken the King's shilling" in their beer, been deemed to have joined the Army. However, the circumstances of the last years of the century led Austria to introduce conscription in 1868, and the German Empire to do the same when it was set up in 1871. Italy followed suit in 1873, and Russia in 1874. At the same time, a series of wars involving European Powers led to the growth of larger and larger armies. By the time of the First World War, the Russian Army alone had between two and three million men under arms, with Germany and France not far behind. Even Britain's "contemptible little army" (as the German Emperor described it) of 150,000 men quickly grew to 2 million in the period 1914-1916.

During this period British governments faced repeated alarms, despite the fact that Britain, by virtue of its large Navy and extensive colonies, was the Superpower of the age. A number of the crises related to the Near East, where the decline of the Turkish Empire and the growing ambitions of Russia threatened the British route to the key colony of India. In 1875 reports in the British press that the Cabinet had discussed the possibility of conscription led Brother Robert Roberts to write:

> "... this may be the closing trial of the brethren of Christ who must go to prison or to death before they violate the ... precepts of their ... Master against taking the sword."

FROM CIVIL WAR TO WORLD WAR

This crisis, and another in 1878, led to a decision to petition Parliament via the Liberal leader William Gladstone. Not all brethren and sisters approved of this proposal, since some felt it was better not to draw attention to our stand, and others perhaps were uneasy about using the civil right of petitioning a Parliament, whose sovereignty over the people of God was denied where it ran counter to the commandments of Christ. In the event the crisis passed, and the petition was not presented. The text is of interest, however, since it set out several important principles.

Christadelphian Petition

It began by stressing the Christadelphian belief in the kingdom of God to be set up on earth on the return of Jesus, and then referred in some detail to the New Testament commandments against war, with paraphrases of Scripture which most Members of Parliament of that time would be sure to recognise. The petition then made reference to Christadelphian consistency as conscientious objectors, quoting the example of petitions during the American Civil War to back up this claim. Finally, and less nobly, the petition stated that Christadelphians were "few in number ... and not likely to be rapidly increased ... The granting of the petition will in no degree embarrass the military measures (taken)." This clause was omitted in later petitions.

The stress upon the Scriptural foundation of our stand and the consistency with which it was held became a hallmark of all subsequent appeals for exemption from military service.

A DEVOUT SOLDIER

During the late 19th Century, when the number of converts was rising rapidly, it was not uncommon for men serving in the army to respond to the truth and be baptized. The experiences of one such brother were recounted in *The Christadelphian* of June 1901, recalling the case of Cornelius (Acts 10:7,8):

> DEAR BROTHER, I daresay you can imagine what an awkward predicament I find myself in at present. When I joined the Army I thought it was an honourable calling, and a matter of duty to fight for one's native country. However ... the politics and wars of the present dark and deluded world are of the world, therefore must be

THE CAPTIVE CONSCIENCE

left alone by Christ's brethren, who are not of the world. If I were able, I would leave the Army now, but I am sorry to say that I cannot do so just yet.

This is not the only reason why the Army has lost its charms for me. For instance, it is difficult to study God's Holy Word in such a place as this. A barrack-room is by no means a fit place for such a sacred study, surrounded, as one is, by noise, fighting, swearing, filthy language, songs, and jokes, and blaspheming of everything connected with God ... It is only by prayer and the daily reading of the Bible, the Commandments of Christ, and other books that I have, that I am able to keep up my faith, which at the best of times, is much too weak. The articles in *The Christadelphian* are also instrumental in cheering and comforting me, especially the exhortations; also the letters from - - - - are very welcome and helpful.

There is another reason why army service is objectionable to a Christadelphian. This is the fact that the only religions recognised in the service are Roman Catholic, Church of England, and Wesleyan. It is needless to say that we know these are all wrong. Every soldier must attend one of these services, whether he likes it or not ... However, I am convinced that their teachings will in no wise alter my opinion of these religions. All the while I have the testimony of the Bible to prove that they are hopelessly wrong, although at the same time I should like to be where I could hear the Gospel of the Kingdom preached in all sincerity and simplicity by men who have been persuaded "out of the Law and the Prophets", and not by popular theological fables and superstitions.

DEAR BROTHER, I wish to acknowledge the receipt of your kind letter of the 20th, and also of the books by a later post of the same date. Perhaps it will interest you to know that, since last writing, I have interviewed my commanding officer, with a view to obtaining my discharge ... However, I must patiently await further developments. As you truly say in your letter, God can open a way for me if I hold fast, for although things seem impossible to us, with God all things are possible; and often the greatest trials and difficulties are blessings in disguise. I must do the best I can, and trust in God to bring me out of the difficulty I am in at present. If, however, I am called upon to fight, I know my duty to Christ, and he will help me to hold fast the "profession of my faith without wavering".[*]

It was during the South African War in 1899-1902 that the question of conscription again became a significant issue. The British Army was frustrated by the tactics of the Boers (the Afrikaans word for farmers) and their superior

---

[*] The brother was subsequently discharged in 1902.

knowledge of the South African countryside, and worried by the rejection on grounds of ill-health of a third of those who volunteered. Newspaper comment at the time led Brother C. C. Walker, who had become editor of *The Christadelphian* on the death of Brother Robert Roberts in 1898, to comment in *The Christadelphian* on the likely use of conscription in the "next war" and to publish a series of articles in 1900 which were later printed in pamphlet form as *Christ and War*. This led to a further proposal for a petition to Parliament. The text was similar to that of 1878 and, after it had appeared in *The Christadelphian* (1903, page 76), forty ecclesias signed the petition, and Lord Morpeth, MP agreed

Part of the Petition drafted in 1903

to present it; but the crisis passed and the petition was withdrawn.

By 1913, war between Britain, France and Russia on one side, and Germany and Austria-Hungary on the other, seemed increasingly likely. In the British colonies of Australia and New Zealand conscription had already been introduced. Newspapers reported that young men who objected were being imprisoned. This sufficiently alarmed a number of brethren in South London to lead them to suggest a further petition to Parliament. The Lincoln ecclesia had already done this on its own, and now another 150 ecclesias signed the new petition.

When the petition was prepared there were still many who hoped war might be avoided; but by the time it was presented to Parliament in February 1915, Europe was already engulfed in war. The fact that the preparation of the petition preceded the outbreak of war helped counter the charge that it was a cowards' charter but, in the patriotic fervour of late 1914, it was difficult to find a member of Parliament willing to present it. Eventually Arnold Rowntree, Member of Parliament for York, a Quaker, agreed to do so.

Three things were stressed in the petition: firstly, our belief in the Second Coming of Jesus to rule over the earth; secondly, the teaching of the Lord Jesus and the apostles against the use of force against enemies; and, thirdly, the consistent and well documented stand of the community against military service, since its earliest days. In addition, our willingness to obey the laws of the land when not in conflict with God's Law was also stressed, and reference made to praying for God's guidance for the Government. When it was presented recruitment was still voluntary. It would not be until 1916, when the supply of volunteers had been consumed on the muddy fields of France, that brethren would meet their sternest test, demonstrating the importance of the earlier petitions and other written evidence of the Christadelphian objection to military service.

6

"YOUR KING AND COUNTRY NEED YOU!"

WHEN the First World War (known until 1939 as "The Great War") broke out, it was accompanied by a patriotic fervour, accentuated by indignation against the Germans for attacking "gallant little Belgium" in accordance with the Schlieffen Plan, by which the Germans bypassed the French defences. Cartoons of the time showed Germany as a vicious Prussian bully attacking a brave boy.

Tales of atrocities perpetrated by the advancing Germans filled the newspapers, and a huge recruiting campaign went

BRAVO, BELGIUM!

THE CAPTIVE CONSCIENCE

into action. Popular music-hall stars of the day sang songs such as this:

> "We've watched you playing cricket,
> And every kind of game,
> At football, golf and polo
> You men have made your name.
> But now your country calls you
> To play your part in war,
> And no matter what befalls you
> We shall love you all the more!
> So come and join the forces
> As your fathers did before ...
>
> Oh, we don't want to lose you,
> But we think you ought to go,
> For your King and your Country
> Both need you so.
> We shall want you and miss you,
> But with all our might and main,
> We shall cheer you, thank you, kiss you,
> When you come back again!"
>
> PAUL RUBENS

Backed by the famous Kitchener poster (reproduced alongside), and with queues of young men at recruiting offices anxious not to miss the fighting, such propaganda must have made standing out as conscientious objectors very difficult for young brethren, especially when some young women took to challenging young men not in uniform by giving them white feathers.

The Young Worker's Advocate and Mutual Magazine, a Christadelphian

"YOUR KING AND COUNTRY NEED YOU!" publication for young brethren, took a different view of the recuitment campaign:

Young Christadelphian: "Ah! I wonder how long it will be before MY King and Country need ME? Not long, I hope."

The same publication commented that by late 1915:

" ... in many quarters, such as workshops and public offices the moral pressure (to join the Army) brought to bear has been almost equal to compulsion." (page 142)

Sadly this pressure sometimes led to brethren abandoning their stand, as the following item of intelligence in *The Christadelphian* in late 1914 shows:

"With deep regret I have to report that we have been compelled to withdraw from - - - - in consequence of their attitude on the question of military service. Brother - - - - enlisted in the army for active service, and is quite unable to see or admit that he has done wrong, and all the four brethren, and sister - - - - take up the attitude that the present war is a righteous one, and that

THE CAPTIVE CONSCIENCE

> Christ's commandments do not forbid the bearing of arms and fighting in defence of King and Country, failing to grasp the fact that the weapons of our warfare are not carnal."

Such desertions were a bitter blow, particularly to small ecclesias.

Church Attitudes

The attitude of the churches to the war was generally one of loyalty and patriotism. Indeed, as in the Middle Ages, the notion of the just war was often advanced to justify the killing. The then Bishop of Durham spoke of the "holiness of patriotism," and the Bishop of London was reckoned to have influenced at least one hundred thousand men to volunteer. The Rector of a London parish argued that:

> "There was never a truer patriot than Christ …"

Whilst some clergymen argued that the war should be fought "with clean hands", others openly applauded hostility to conscientious objectors, and called for sterner penalties for them once conscription had been introduced. Such attitudes made the differences between Christadelphians and the established churches all the more evident.

Towards Conscription

By 1916 the number of volunteers was diminishing, as the casualties mounted in the trenches of Flanders and Northern France. The first day of the battle of the Somme in July 1916 saw 60,000 killed or injured. Although the military censors tried to keep the worst of the details from the British public, the grim daily lists in the newspapers of those killed and injured told of a terrible price being paid in young lives. Worst of all, in the first years of the war, some young men had been encouraged to join "Old Pals' Battalions", made up of groups of youngsters from the same town or even the same streets. Heavy losses amongst such battalions were devastating to their home towns, and led to this policy being abandoned. Lord Derby was appointed to set up committees to help recruit replacements, but the toll was too great for volunteers to fill the gaps.

It was therefore no surprise when conscription was eventually introduced. It had been preceded by the National Registration Act of 1915, which required everyone between

"YOUR KING AND COUNTRY NEED YOU!"

the ages of 15 and 65, except those already in the Army and Navy, to be registered. In addition, the Act required *men* to give the kind of information which would be essential to the operation of conscription: for example, it asked them to say whether they were married, single or widowed, how many young children they had, and what employment they were in. At the same time the Derby recruitment drive encouraged men to attest their willingness to serve their country. A popular rumour that only those who did this would be allowed civilian rather than military service led to a few brethren mistakenly attesting. Most, however, resisted the enormous pressures brought to bear.

The Introduction of Conscription

The Military Service Bill of 1916 was introduced into Parliament in January, with the proposal to conscript single men and childless widowers aged 18-40. By the time it became law in May 1916, this had changed to the conscription of all men between 18 and 41, with single men being called up first. This Act included the right to object on grounds of conscience; an answer to the fervent prayer of those who had put forward the petition of 1915.

Military Service Act 1916

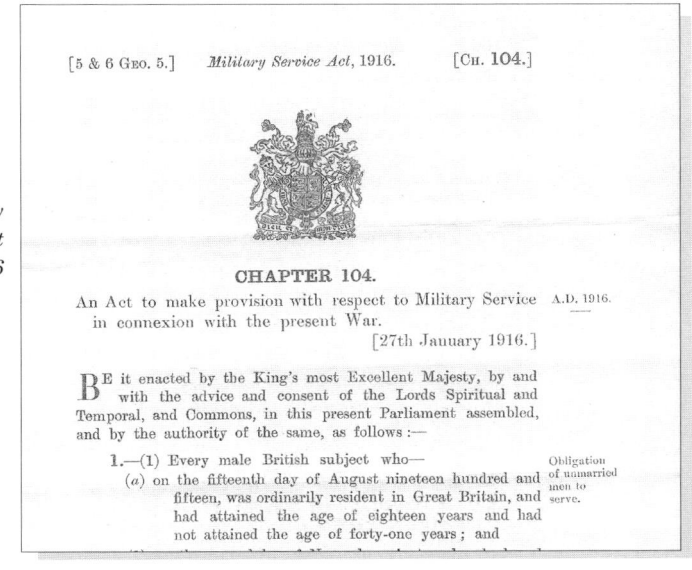

THE CAPTIVE CONSCIENCE

The petition was fully described in *The Christadelphian* early in 1916:

THE Bill at present before the House of Commons concerning Compulsory Military Service provides for Certificates of Exemption on four grounds: (1) that of more useful employment to the nation than in the army; (2) that a man is the sole support of dependents; (3) ill-health or infirmity; (4) conscientious objections.

It is the last that so deeply concerns us. The London Committee of brethren have done their best in the premises. On December 8th they issued a report of progress to date, which report was sent from the office of *The Christadelphian* to British readers of the magazine a day or two in advance of the January issue ... The London Committee wish it to be understood that the report sent out should be circulated as widely as possible among the ecclesias.

The subjoined precis was prepared by the Committee for the information of the Prime Minister and members of the Cabinet:

WE, THE CHRISTADELPHIANS IN GREAT BRITAIN, HEREBY HUMBLY CLAIM THE RIGHTS AND PRIVILEGES OF ABSOLUTE TOTAL EXEMPTION FROM MILITARY SERVICE AS GRACIOUSLY ARRANGED FOR UNDER CLAUSE 2 (1) (d) OF THE "MILITARY SERVICE (NO. 2) BILL" NOW BEFORE THE GOVERNMENT, AND IN SUPPORT OF SUCH HUMBLY SUBMIT THE FOLLOWING DESCRIPTIVE PARTICULARS FOR YOUR GRACIOUS CONSIDERATION.

1. The title, "Christadelphian", was adopted in 1865 as a distinctive appellation for a body of believers who, for religious reasons, were seeking exemption from military service at the outbreak of the American Civil War.

2. The "Christadelphian" tenets in relation to the State require them in the fear of God to honour the King, to be subject to all rulers and magistrates, to live in peaceable submission to, and strict observance of, the Laws of the Realm, save only should those laws contravene the commandments of Christ, which, they hold, require them, as being in the world but not of it, to consistently abstain from participation in politics and from military service.

3. In holding this conscientious objection (a) to military service, and (b) in seeking to be legally exempt therefrom, they are not adopting any new attitude; their literature for the past fifty years is evidence of this.

On the first point (a) the following citation from the magazine called *The Christadelphian* (for 1872, page 489) is pertinent:

"If we must pay heavy penalties, unless we choose to break the law of God, let the penalties be paid. If we must be killed and our families with us, unless we forfeit the approbation of our Lord and Master, and lose eternal life at his coming, let us die at once: we are

"YOUR KING AND COUNTRY NEED YOU!"

not to consider consequences at all ... It is a mistake to hamper the question of duty with any secondary conditions whatever".

On the second point (b) the evidence shows that in 1878 a petition was drawn up, and that Mr. Gladstone consented to present it. And again in 1904, Lord Morpeth undertook a similar favour on our behalf. Doubts as to the suitability of the time kept the matter in abeyance, but in 1913 (eight months before the present war) it was pursued in a more decided manner, resulting in the presentation, through the kindly offices of Mr. Arnold Rowntree, MP, in February of last year, of the Petition which now awaits your gracious consideration.

4. We respectfully beg to state that our community is not such as could be suddenly augmented by those merely desirous of escaping compulsory military service. We are what might be termed an exclusive community. None is admitted who has not, in a lengthy interview, satisfied specially appointed and responsible elders that they are exactly at one with us on a large number of particular doctrines, and that they will in matter of practice adorn the cause they wish to espouse.

Our registers are well-kept, and the names of those who cease to maintain the correct faith or attitude are expunged therefrom, so that we have an attested membership easily capable of proof.

5. In no way do we desire to embarrass the Government by our attitude; the smallness of our numbers excludes the possibility of this.

6. We are not seeking ease and comfort when others are suffering, but only that freedom may be graciously accorded us to be obedient to what we believe to be the commands of the All-wise God, who, we know, is working out in this present trying war His divine purpose of eventual good.

Signed on behalf of the said Christadelphians: J. M. EVANS, F. G. JANNAWAY, G. F. LAKE, H. E. PURSER, W. A. SIMPER, A. S. THOMPSON, W. H. TRAPP, The London Standing Committee, Clapham Public Hall, High Street, Clapham, London, S.W.   January 14, 1915

The group of South London brethren who had promoted the petition, of whom Brother Frank Jannaway became the most well-known, had not been idle. Now augmented by additional members, the London Standing Committee, as it was called, had written to the Prime Minister, Mr. Asquith, and his Cabinet ministers, to remind them of the Christadelphian position. Their letter reminded the Government of our abstention from politics and military service. It stressed that the careful interviewing of candidates for baptism made it difficult for anyone to join our community in order to escape conscription, and pointed out that careful registers were kept of membership and attendance, to identify clearly genuine Christadelphians. *To all who have wondered why we have ecclesial registrars, the importance of this point in reassuring the Government of the time cannot be over-emphasized.* The work of the Committee in advising and informing brethren on how they should react was equally valuable, which is why a Military Service Committee continues to exist to this day. Letters were sent frequently to ecclesias and individual brethren, with invaluable advice.

Another brother who was particularly active was Viner Hall, a Birmingham brother of strong convictions. He had been active in opposing a proposal from the Birmingham Temperance Hall ecclesia for a petition which appeared to suggest that brethren would be willing to undertake noncombatant National Service, and he seems to have influenced the London Standing Committee. He also suggested a statement which brethren might use when faced with the National Registration Act of 1915:

"Below is a suggested form of affidavit for the use of brethren in the event of their being called upon to engage in Military Service:

'I, A.B., do conscientiously believe all wars, fightings, and fleshly strivings, to be contrary to the letter and spirit of the law of Christ. As a Christadelphian, or brother of Christ, I cannot therefore under *any* circumstances join the ranks of those that make war; neither can I conscientiously engage in any form or branch of military service; nor in any employment or form of service necessitating constant Sunday work which would prevent or interfere with my service of Christ in the Gospel; nor in any service whatsoever, which might involve the use of force or resort to arms, or necessitate me taking the Military Oath or Affirmation. On these grounds I ask you to grant me a legal exemption from Military Service according to the statute etc.' "

He followed this up with a powerful exhortation:

THE RIGHT IS BEST

"Whatever is right is best. That is the first axiom of faith in God. Best now and best hereafter, best from the point of view of expediency and tactics as well as best from the point of ultimate results,

"YOUR KING AND COUNTRY NEED YOU!"

if only we could see far enough and clearly enough; and surely, brethren, we who have had the eyes of our understanding opened by God can see far enough and clearly enough! Brethren, the path of safety, of sanity, of salvation, is faith in God! Believe and obey. Do His will *and take the consequences.* Be sure that those consequences will be the best for you and the world. He that would save his life shall certainly lose it, but he that will lose his life for my sake shall save it.

Faithfully your brother in Christ,

Viner Hall"

(Taken from *Exemption*—the collected papers of Brother Viner Hall by Peter Reekie, page 36.)

The Provisions of the Military Service Act of 1916

The Act allowed exemption from military service on a number of grounds. Firstly, those employed in civilian work regarded as vital, such as coal-miners and steel-workers, could be exempted. Later on such occupations came to be described as reserved occupations. Secondly, exemption could be granted in cases of severe financial, business or family hardship, although this exemption seems to have been rarely more than temporary. Thirdly, those who failed the medical test for recruits were exempted on grounds of ill-health. Finally, provision was made for exemption to be granted on grounds of conscientious objection, following consideration by a Local Tribunal.

Within this final category, exemption could be *absolute*, that is complete and unconditional; *conditional*, that is, on condition that the applicant agreed to do work "of national importance"; or restricted to exemption from combatant service only. This last meant that the applicant had to join a group such as the Royal Army Medical Corps or the Army Service Section, which was responsible for pay, etc. Such non-combatant groups wore uniforms, came under military discipline, and were regarded as being under the same oaths of allegiance as combatants. This last point was an important factor in Christadelphian objections to non-combatant service.

The London Standing Committee advised brethren to claim absolute exemption, but accepted conditional exemption in practice. There seems to have been some confusion in the minds of the Committee and some Tribunals over the exact usage of the terms "absolute" and "conditional", since the Committee referred to some brethren gaining absolute exemption when they were clearly receiving conditional exemption. Some brethren such as Viner Hall felt that only absolute exemption should be accepted, but in practice, absolute exemption seems to have been rarely granted by Tribunals to *any* objector.

The Act also provided for appeals against the ruling of the local tribunal to an Area Appeals Tribunal and, if the applicant for exemption was still not satisfied with the verdict, to a Central Appeals Tribunal in London made up mainly of members of both Houses of Parliament. However, this final appeal could only be made if the Area Appeals Tribunal granted leave to appeal. This mechanism proved important in determining the outcome of applications by brethren in the First World War.

The Question of Non-Combatant Service

The London Standing Committee took a firm stand against the views of those who argued that non-combatant service was acceptable. This stand was based on two key issues:

1. These services all came under military authority, which involved real or implied oaths of loyalty to the Crown.

2. In the last analysis, all those under military authority were seen as part of the military machine, and would also be expected to fight in an emergency.

The second point was very clearly illustrated in the *Manual of Royal Army Medical Corps Training*, which stated:

" ... the medical service must be regarded as part of an organisation which is maintained for the special purpose of fighting ... Medical personnel may have to carry arms for the defence of sick and wounded in (their) charge and for (their) own protection."

Some RAMC men were also transferred to the infantry during the course of the war.

The London Standing Committee therefore advised young brethren to seek absolute exemption from military service.

"YOUR KING AND COUNTRY NEED YOU!"

When challenged on why non-combatant service was unacceptable, the usual reply was:

"I am prepared to sacrifice all material things, to do almost any kind of work under civilian control, but not military, as I cannot promise unqualified obedience to anyone."

To have sworn loyalty to the Crown and accepted military discipline would have seriously undermined the basis of the claim made for exemption.

The Tribunals in Practice

The Act seemed to provide substantial protection to conscientious objectors, but in practice the Tribunals made life very difficult for those who wished to object. Originally intended to consist of only five local dignitaries, some ran to 19 members! What was even worse was that these men were often the self-same local dignitaries who had made up the Lord Derby recruiting committees of the year before. Many of them found it difficult to see their role as anything other than a means of forcing objectors into the Army. Consequently, a good many brethren were only exempted from combatant service, and were likely to be arrested when they failed to report to the military authorities.

The *Young Worker's Advocate and Mutual Magazine* chronicled some of the experiences of brethren during the Spring of 1916:

BRISTOL

"Five more of our brethren appeared on Tuesday, March 21st, asking for total exemption to Military Service. One obtained total exemption (he works on the railway), but the others were ordered to non-combatant service. Notice of appeal was given by the four brethren."

RUGBY

"A Christadelphian was asked by Mr. Loverock if it would not be obeying the commands of Christ to help the wounded? — Applicant said he would do anything in a civil capacity, but he could not take the military oath.

Mr. Loverock — Is it not a case of fear and funk with you rather than of conscience? — Applicant denied this, and said he was willing to put up with the consequences of his objection.

Exemption from combative service only was granted." — *Birmingham Daily Post*, March 17th.

THE CAPTIVE CONSCIENCE

BOURNEMOUTH

"On the grounds that warfare is contrary to their beliefs, eight brethren (with a large body of elderly brethren) appeared in order to ask for absolute exemption. Brother Fry acted as their mouthpiece, and enunciated the principles of our beliefs. Military service, he said, he and his friends could not conscientiously undertake, because it was against the commands of Christ. They did not object to obeying the commands of those set in authority over them, but where these commands were against the commands of Christ they could not obey.

That means that you are a law unto yourselves?—No! Christ's law. Yes! it means that you are a law unto yourselves, so far as it suits you.—We obey man-made laws so long as they are not against the laws of Christ; military service means that we should obey military officers, and we are not prepared to do this. To undertake military service, in our judgement, would be to set at nought the principles of Christ, and in refusing to do this we are following the example of the first and second century Christians …

The military officer observed that Peter had carried a sword in the Garden of Gethsemane, and the spokesman replied that, for using it, the disciple had been rebuked. The Chairman remarked that everyone in these times ought to put their conscience in their pockets, and do something to bring about a speedy victory.

Answering further questions, the applicant stated that all the eight men had long been members of the Christadelphian Society. The Tribunal exempted the applicants from combatant service."

In all these cases appeals were lodged, as the Act permitted, but many of these upheld the original verdict. In one case at least the Area Appeal Court ordered that non-combatant status should be reversed to combatant status! As a result a number of brethren were arrested, court-martialled and imprisoned.

A Lesson for Today

There is a lesson to be learned in all this. Whatever the law may say, the high emotions of wartime or other crises may cause men and women to ignore legal niceties. We seem at the present to be guaranteed exemption on grounds of conscience in Britain and many other parts of the world. But as the circumstances of the final crisis of this world develop, it may well be that such laws will be ignored. Despite Paul's Roman citizenship, the Jews would have happily ignored the law given the opportunity!

"YOUR KING AND COUNTRY NEED YOU!"

It may also be the case that the laws of the land would be changed very quickly in the face of national emergency, especially since the type of legislation adopted in wartime often includes clauses which allow the government to make regulations by decree if it is felt necessary.

There are also some parts of the world, including countries in Eastern Europe, where the rights of conscientious objectors are not recognised in law, and brethren face persecution in time of war or national crisis.

Rampant nationalism is a powerful and frightening force. Are we as ready as some of our brethren of the First World War were to suffer for our Faith?

Negotiations with the Government

The London Standing Committee had not been idle during this time, sending out a succession of circulars to advise on completing the forms for the tribunals, how to respond to the arrival of call up papers and even how brethren should respond to attempts to make them wear military uniform by taking away their clothes!

Towards the end of March a speech by a member of parliament sympathetic to the plight of conscientious objectors, and the government response, suggested a new tactic to the Committee. They wrote to the Government making clear the willingness of the community to "place our services at the disposal of the State in any direction needed, but not as part of the Army or in any combatant or non-combatant capacity".[1] Another member of parliament was also persuaded to raise the issue of Christadelphians in military prisons.

As a result of this, talks took place between Brother Frank Jannaway (who had been a leading figure in the Committee) and various Government ministers. These led first to the release of arrested brethren, pending the hearing of a test-case before the Central Appeal Tribunal.

The Test-Case of April, 1916

Because of the difficulties which had arisen as a result of the refusal of local and some appeals tribunals to grant exemption to brethren, despite the legal requirements of the Act, the Government was persuaded to allow a "Test Case" to be heard by the Central Appeal Tribunal. Their judgement then set a precedent which was to be legally binding on the less powerful local and area-based appeal tribunals.

Brother Charles Gordon Ramsden, whose appeal became the Test Case, was a member of a small Christadelphian group which later became part of the Suffolk Street fellowship.

The statement in support of his application was the one drafted by Brother Viner Hall in February 1916, reproduced below. Brother Ramsden applied for absolute exemption, without conditions.

BROTHER GORDON RAMSDEN'S APPLICATION FOR EXEMPTION

"The servant of the Lord must not strive; but be gentle to all men."
"The weapons of our warfare are not carnal."
(2 Tim. 2:24; 2 Cor. 10:3-5)

TO THE MEMBERS OF THE TRIBUNAL

Gentlemen,

In obedience to the command of the Government, I am here before you to state the grounds of my conscientious objection to Military Service.

By Military Service I mean Military Service in the widest sense of the term; that is to say, every form of service involving the taking of the Military Oath, or Affirmation, or Attestation, or its equivalent, under the Military Authorities in connection with war, or war work.

My conscientious objection to Military Service is the result of a deep religious conviction that *wars, fightings, and fleshly strivings, are contrary to the letter and spirit of the Law of Christ,* as expressed in the "Sermon on the Mount", and amplified in the writings of the Apostles, by which I, as a Christadelphian, or brother of Christ, am bound.

To me, war is the absolute negation of every principle of the doctrine of Christ. Under no circumstances therefore, could I join the ranks of those who make war—BE THE CONSEQUENCES WHAT THEY MAY—not even as a so-called "non-combatant", because there is no difference morally speaking between the man who strikes and the one who helps him to strike.

The combatant and non-combatant are both alike *"integral parts of an organisation which is kept for the special purpose of fighting"*. They are essential to one another; in fact, one is the complement of

"YOUR KING AND COUNTRY NEED YOU!"

the other. They belong to the same body, are subject to the same law, and are under the same oath, which involves a solemn undertaking to fight for King and Country.

The combatant slays while the non-combatant is under obligation to do so in virtue of the oath he has taken, and if necessity arises may be transferred to a combatant regiment.

My conscientious objection to combatant service, therefore, equally holds good in regard to so-called non-combatant service.

On these grounds, and under these special and exceptional circumstances, I respectfully beg to claim a complete and unconditional certificate of exemption from Military Service, which you have the power to grant, and to which I am entitled in virtue of the provisions of the Act relating to conscientious objectors, as interpreted and explained by Mr. Long in the Local Government Board instructions issued on February 4th, 1916, explaining the application and effect of the Act, where it expressly states that "in exceptional cases in which the genuine convictions and circumstances of the man are such that neither exemption from combatant service nor a conditional exemption will adequately meet the case, absolute exemption may be granted in these cases if the tribunal are fully satisfied of the facts"—a provision which gives effect to the assurance of Mr. Asquith, in his speech reported on January 6th, that the Government had taken every care to "secure that no one shall come under the obligation created by the Bill unless it is manifest he has no reasonable ground for not responding to his Country's Call".

The application was rejected and Gordon Ramsden was issued with a certificate for service in a non-combatant corps. He appealed to the London Appeal Tribunal, and only 8 weeks later was summoned to appear before a Committee of 25 politicians, military and civic dignitaries held in Committee Room 9 at the Houses of Parliament on March 13th, 1916 with over 100 members of the public in attendance. The atmosphere was heavily charged—the politicians on the Tribunal looking over their shoulders at the potential reactions to their verdict. Their decision was that he was exempt from front-line duty but not from non-combatant service.

This was not acceptable to Brother Gordon, so a further appeal was made to the Central Tribunal—the highest court of appeal in Whitehall—on the grounds that already having given his allegiance to his King and Saviour, the Lord Jesus Christ, Gordon could afford no allegiance to the king of

England, nor could he subject himself to military control, even in a non-combatant role.

The Central Appeal Tribunal chairman was the Marquess of Salisbury and it comprised about ten other Members of Parliament and also military representatives. They considered many documents including different Christadelphian magazines and a Statement of Faith dated 1883 wherein it was stated that "We take no part in politics, nor join the Army or Navy".

The decision of this Tribunal was to grant exemption subject to Brother Ramsden being engaged in "work which, not being under military control, is nevertheless useful for the prosecution of the War." This last phrase caused considerable disquiet amongst brethren and sisters, but Brother Frank Jannaway was afterwards able to secure clarification that the phrase simply meant "work of National Importance".

In private the Tribunal seems to have accepted the request for absolute exemption, and a subsequent letter from the Tribunal invited the London Standing Committee "to state what Civil work Christadelphians were prepared to undertake". The discrepancy between the public and private versions seems to have reflected the Government's desire not to draw attention to the very special exemption being granted as a result of the Test Case to all subsequent Christadelphian applicants for exemption.

After the success of the Test Case, Brother Frank Jannaway was given the opportunity of intervening directly with the War Office to secure the release of those whose appeals had been refused by lower courts. This often infuriated local tribunals, who did everything they could to reverse such decisions.

These problems led in turn to the establishment of a register of *bona fide* Christadelphians compiled by Brother Frank Jannaway for the War Office, and later to the issue of Certificates of Exemption to all young brethren, to ensure they could no longer be called up. In addition, Brother Frank Jannaway entered into a personal bond of £10,000, guaranteeing that the system would not be abused.

"YOUR KING AND COUNTRY NEED YOU!"

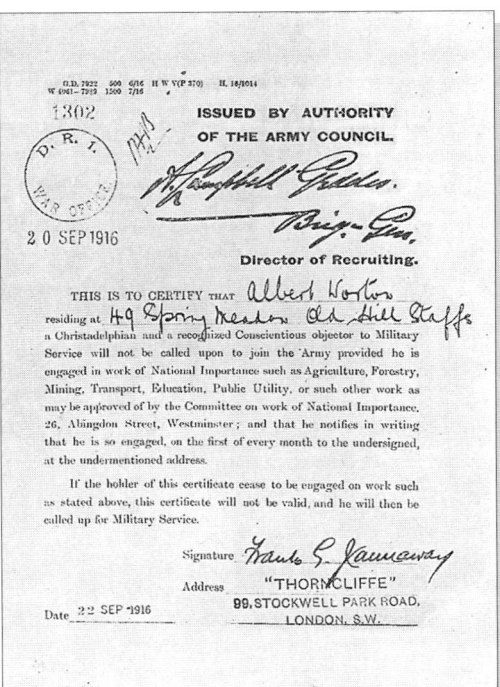

A Certificate of Exemption

A Privileged Position

In all, over 16,500 men objected to military service on grounds of conscience in the First World War, including some 1,400 Christadelphians. Only the Christadelphian community was allowed the privilege of a Certificate of Exemption. Why was this?

Firstly, the consistency with which the Christadelphian position was held clearly impressed Government Ministers.

Secondly, the willingness of brethren to suffer rather than give up their conviction was recognised as a measure of their strength of conscience. Those in military prisons were especially at risk, being imprisoned in draughty barrack cells with planks to sleep on and plank ends as pillows. Some were subjected not only to verbal abuse, but also to physical abuse. One spent over four months in prison, having his clothes torn off, being beaten on several occasions, often having only bread and water, and being subjected to humiliating treatment in front of the whole regiment. Another was marched through the town clad only in a blanket, having refused to put on a uniform. Yet faith held fast, helped by such things as the Bible Classes held by Brother Frank Jannaway in Wormwood Scrubs Prison (where at one time 15 brethren were confined), visits by other brethren, and the letters and prayers of the whole community.

Certificate from the Committee on Work of National Importance

Work of National Importance

A condition of this special position was that single brethren and some married brethren were required to find work of National Importance. A Government committee set out to help find work of this kind for objectors. It was not a popular task.

No definitive list of occupations coming under this heading was published by the Committee, but Brother Frank Jannaway did obtain an unpublished list which gives clear indications of what was acceptable:

"YOUR KING AND COUNTRY NEED YOU!"
COMMITTEE ON WORK OF NATIONAL IMPORTANCE

Preliminary List of Occupations which the Committee recommend to the Tribunals as being of National Importance

AGRICULTURE—Farm Labour, Market Gardening, Fruit Growing, Seed Raising, Agriculture Machinery, Making and Repairing, Agricultural Education and Organisation.

FORESTRY—Cutting, Hauling and Preparing Timber.

SHIPPING—Mercantile Marine, Ship Building and Repairing.

TRANSPORT—Railways and Canals, Docks and Wharves, Cartage connected with the same.

EDUCATION

PUBLIC UTILITY SERVICE—Sanitary Services (Local Authorities), Fire Brigades, Civil Hospitals, Workhouses, Infirmaries, Asylums.

RED CROSS AND GENERAL WELFARE WORK—Ambulance Work at home and abroad, Welfare Work. In certain cases objectors who have special qualifications might be allowed to engage in welfare work in Camp and Munition Factories, or in Orderly work in Internment Camps.

The above list of occupations has been drawn up with a view to indicating work which conscientious objectors to Military Service might be permitted to undertake.

In a number of cases men who are not available for active military service, may, with most advantage to the nation, be employed in the class of work in which they are already engaged, but as a general rule it may be expedient that an applicant should not be allowed to remain under the same employer, and, in some cases, a change of locality may be advisable.

There are some occupations involving special qualifications, such as medical and other professional work, including that of medical students, where it would be uneconomical to remove a man from his existing work.

The Committee recommend that as a general rule an applicant should not be transferred to work which could suitably be undertaken by a woman, unless the applicant's physical condition makes such a course advisable. They consider that he should not be transferred to an employment by which he will make a financial gain.

The Committee have not included in the above list "Iron and Steel Works", or other similar works of great National Importance which are primarily "Munition Works".

The Committee are informed that the Labour Exchanges are prepared to assist in finding suitable vacancies in the occupations mentioned in the list.

THE CAPTIVE CONSCIENCE

The Committee are taking steps to ascertain where individual applicants can most suitably be placed, and will further advise Tribunals as, and when, applications are referred to the Committee.

All communications should be addressed to: The Secretary, Committee on Work of National Importance, 26, Abingdon Street, Westminster, London, S.W.

Working on the Land

Many brethren tried to find work on the land, where the loss of men to the war meant that there were often vacancies, in an age when mechanisation was very limited. Brethren found their lives much changed, with days sometimes as long as from 5.30 am to 10.30 pm in the summer. However, most adapted well to the task, and on more than one occasion, Brother Frank Jannaway was contacted by a farmer asking if he could "at once send three more young Christadelphians like the one you sent last month". Learning to milk by hand was not easy, nonetheless, and agricultural wages were usually lower than those the brethren had previously earned. Others went into forestry, some to the railways; and a good many married men were allowed to remain in their existing work after the London Standing Committee had suggested that putting them into

"YOUR KING AND COUNTRY NEED YOU!"

low-paid work would only lead to them having to seek Parish relief to help support their families, thus putting more burden on the State.

Work in Arms Manufacture

One occupation caused considerable concern. A number of brethren were engaged in manufacturing guns, shells or other armaments. In many cases this was because peacetime engineering factories had altered production to munitions at the start of the war, although a few seem to have been attracted by the high wages.

Such men attracted considerable comment from the tribunals, and were often refused exemption. The Lord Mayor of Birmingham, sitting on a tribunal at which Brother C. C. Walker was appearing for a number of young brethren, including some in munitions, commented that he "could not understand the logic of the position which objected to a man using weapons in self-defence, but had no objection to making shells".

An otherwise sympathetic tribunal chairman in Coventry made a similar point: "We cannot understand how a body that holds the beliefs … that by the laws of God they cannot take part in war … can on the one hand disenfranchise, if that is the right word, a man who fires off a gun, and keeps as a member a man who makes the gun and refuses to fire it off".

Not surprisingly, those who were engaged in making armaments found it more difficult to obtain exemption. Because of this the London Standing Committee repeatedly wrote to young brethren with a very clear message:

"CHOOSE THOSE OCCUPATIONS FURTHEST REMOVED FROM MUNITIONS WORK."

Such advice must remain sound common sense, even though the issue was left to the conscience of individuals in both World Wars.

It was, however, an issue which caused great debate. *The Young Worker's Advocate* suggested that the argument against making munitions could be taken to extremes:

> "Some tribunals insist that in order to be consistent … we ought not to build munitions factories … drive an engine attached to a troop train … If this argument is followed … we ought not to make

soldiers' uniforms ... deliver bread to the barracks ... post a parcel because a percentage of the postal charge is war tax ..."

April 1916, page 99

Whilst such an argument may be allowable in logic, the advice to keep away from any occupations related to the manufacture of weapons of war is a far better way of following the spirit of the commandments of Christ.[2]

A Question of Faith

Since the First World War there have been some doubts expressed about the wisdom of the stand taken in 1916. In particular, the statement that: "Every bone fide Christadelphian ... will do his best in civil life to help the land of his birth in its hour of distress", in the book *Without the Camp*, written by Brother Frank Jannaway, sits uneasily besides such descriptions of true disciples as "aliens and exiles" (1 Peter 2:11, RSV) or the comment in Hebrews that "Here we have no lasting city, but we seek the city which is to come" (Hebrews 13:14, RSV). When the judgements of God are in the earth we must also ask ourselves whether we should be shoring up the institutions of this present age. This issue was to become more critical as civilians became more and more involved in the Second World War, and may well prove to be an issue of life and death in the final crisis of this world.

Nonetheless, the steadfastness of most young brethren in the face of severe testing remains the over-riding impression from the war years of 1914-1918. Many sacrificed a great deal for their Faith, and most would lead lives much changed by their experiences once peace came in 1918. It is also important to remember that the brethren of the London Standing Committee were in a very difficult and fluid situation, and did not have the benefit of hindsight we possess.

A Case of Mistaken Identity!

Even in the Great War, there were moments of humour. One episode recorded in *Without the Camp* illustrates this perfectly:

> "A clayworker said at Ormskirk yesterday that he was a Christadelphian and had a conscientious objection to fighting. On being asked whether he would defend his hearth and home against

"YOUR KING AND COUNTRY NEED YOU!"
Germans he bluntly replied, 'I would not take their lives, but if I got near them, I would give them a smack across the chops'.
The Chairman: 'You are the sort we want.'
The application was refused."—*Lloyd's Weekly*, March 1916
It turned out that the man in question was not, in fact, a Christadelphian!

---

1. The issue of non-combatant service (that is, administrative, medical and nursing service) was one which had caused considerable debate. A petition drawn up in 1914 by the Birmingham Temperance Hall Ecclesia had included a controversial clause allowing non-combatant service, but wiser counsels prevailed and this clause was withdrawn.

2. "Munition-making" is the activity which produces fighting materials, or other materials which would not be required for civilian use in times of peace. Thus weapons, ammunition, military vehicles and aircraft, military uniforms, substances which in preponderant degree are used as explosives in weapons, nuclear material primarily intended for nuclear weapons (rather than for power-generators), chemicals primarily intended as intermediates in the chain of producing weapons and the like, are illustrations of munitions.

Primary agricultural products and chemical products which would be required whether war was in issue or not, such as cotton and synthetic fibres, may not be munitions. The fact that some portion of these materials may at a later stage be modified for the use of military personnel does not render their primary production culpable, since such personnel would need to be clothed and fed whether engaged in military activities or not. The primary production of coal, oil, and other fuels may be judged to be in the same category, but not specialised processes designed to produce derivatives preponderantly for offensive military purposes. Constructional and building materials which would be required for civilian use in times of peace—such as crude iron and steel, bricks, cement, and the like—are not to be classified as munitions even though they could be in various degrees diverted into military use, but the construction of buildings and other structures designed for military purposes is likely to be unacceptable.

Medical supplies and structures, designed for healing, and tending the sick or wounded, should probably not be thought of as munitions, because healing the suffering is in all circumstances a charitable activity. Even the construction of material intended for field-hospitals might be included here.

Obviously there are grey areas, of which many aspects of the aviation industry could be examples. A rule of thumb might be to suspect any such activity which undergoes sudden expansion in times of war.

7

BETWEEN THE WARS

THE First World War came to an end at 11 am on 11th November, 1918. Almost to the end lives were being lost. In all, over 9 million men had died in what in retrospect seemed an increasingly meaningless struggle. The exhausted nations, burdened with debt and economic disruption, quickly fell prey to social upheaval and high unemployment, which culminated in the Great Depression of 1929-34.

In such a climate, the euphoria over the end of the War quickly evaporated. At the end of the war, conscientious objectors were not released from restrictions until August 1919. They were also forbidden to vote for five years, although this was no hardship to our brethren.

As the full realisation of the huge numbers of dead and wounded sank in, and the returning soldiers told of the terrors of the trenches, a strong anti-war movement developed. This reached its peak in the late 1920s and early 1930s with the founding of the Peace Pledge Union. In 1933 the Labour Party passed a motion to "take no part in war". In 1934 Canon Dick Sheppard's appeal to men with pacifist ideals to write to him led to over 50,000 responses. The Peace Pledge Union at its height had over 100,000 supporters in Britain.

Renewed Fears of War

The rise of Fascism, first in Italy, then in Germany, and later in Spain, led to a rapid change of heart during the 1930s. All Fascist governments showed a ruthlessness against opponents, and a military bravado which frightened other European countries. Despite the widespread fear of what a new war might bring, by 1935 there was a growing feeling that a second great war might be inevitable. When in 1936 Hitler's German troops re-occupied the Rhineland, which had been demilitarised after the First World War, and the Spanish Fascists began a rebellion which turned into the Spanish Civil War, many supporters of the Peace Pledge Union abandoned their views in favour of the notion of a just war against evil. Even some of those who had been imprisoned for their conscientious objection to the First World War abandoned their views, and a number of former pacifists fought in the International Brigade of volunteers against the Fascists in Spain. When German "volunteer" pilots bombed Guernica, the wave of moral indignation felt in the non-Fascist European states swept away any remaining doubts concerning the justification for war.

The Military Service Committee, set up in 1935, was intended to take the place of the London Standing Committee, which had been disbanded soon after the First World War. Following a meeting of ecclesial delegates, one of its first acts was to send a letter to all brethren and sisters urging upon them the need for "the avoidance NOW of occupations involving the direct manufacture of instruments used solely for the destruction of human life." Following this advice meant real hardship for any who had been out of work during the Depression of the early 1930s, since rearmament created many thousands of new jobs. But as the war clouds gathered once more over Europe, it was clearly good advice.

8

CONSCIENTIOUS OBJECTION IN THE SECOND WORLD WAR

DESPITE repeated pledges by Governments of the early and middle 1930s not to introduce conscription, it was known that the necessary laws were kept in readiness for a new crisis.

Such a crisis blew up in the summer of 1938, when it was claimed that Germans living in the border area of Czechoslovakia known as the Sudetenland had demanded to be allowed to become part of Hitler's Third Reich, which had just been created by the union of Austria and Germany. The support of Germany for this demand brought Europe to the brink of war, and preparations for defence against attacks by the German air force were hurriedly made, with trenches dug in public parks in  London. Faced by German threats of military action, the other European Powers met at Munich and agreed to the German demands. The British Prime Minister, Neville Chamberlain, returned to Britain claiming that he had secured "peace in our time", but it is doubtful whether even he believed that he had done more than postpone the war, at the expense of the loss of Czech defence lines. When the rest of Czechoslovakia was taken under German "protection" in March 1939, war seemed certain, especially when

THE SECOND WORLD WAR

Europe in 1939. Key: H—Holland; B—Belgium; S—Switzerland; B-M—Bohemia & Moravia; SL—Slovakia; EP—East Prussia

German demands were then switched to large portions of Polish-held territory.

Already in January 1939 a National Service Campaign had been started to encourage recruitment. At the same time a Citizen Service League was set up to lobby for conscription, and in London parks and other open spaces air-raid shelters were hurriedly excavated. Finally, in April 1939 conscription was again introduced. Five months later the Second World War broke out, when the German attack on Poland forced France and Britain to attempt to fulfil the promises they had made to defend that country.

The Christadelphian Military Service Committee acted quickly to ensure that brethren affected by conscription received the right advice. A letter of 1st June warned that all brethren aged 20 and 21 would have to report for registration as conscripts on the following Saturday, June 3rd. Clear guidance was given about how to ask to be enrolled on

55

THE CAPTIVE CONSCIENCE

the register of Conscientious Objectors. The registration was done in alphabetical order, so that some brethren were amongst the first to be considered. Such brethren sometimes found the officials woefully unprepared to deal with conscientious objectors, even though the Act making National Service compulsory was clear. Every person was entitled to state his objection before a specially constituted tribunal, which would decide if his objection was conscientious or not. However, gradually, the mechanisms were put in place, and brethren were summoned to state their case against conscription.

The Work of the Tribunals

Unlike the Tribunals of the First World War, the new tribunals were set up under the control of the Ministry of

Newspaper Headlines just before the Outbreak of War

Labour with the membership scrutinised carefully. The Chairman was usually a County Court judge, who sat with four other members in what was intended to be an impartial hearing, to establish whether the objection of the applicant was genuine or not. Each applicant could be accompanied by a friend, relative or legal representative, a right which brethren were able to use to good purpose. Older brethren who travelled extensively to accompany applicants frequently became known and respected in many of the eleven tribunals in England and Wales and four in Scotland. In

THE SECOND WORLD WAR

Birmingham Brother John Carter accompanied scores of young brethren, whose appearance before the tribunal was substantially eased by his calm and determined presence.

At the outset of the War there were 3,300 applications from conscientious objectors, and delays were considerable, in some cases up to seven months. Later, as the War went against Britain, the numbers fell. These were to be judged on whether their "religious or ethical convictions were honestly held", as Judge Wethered in the South West put it. Another judge stated:

> "We have to ascertain what is in the minds of the applicants, to appraise the genuineness and sincerity of their views, to plumb the depths of their convictions ... by getting to understand *the background of the lives of each of those who come before us* ..." (my emphasis)

This could mean a close examination of the faith and practices of brethren and sisters. Public scrutiny could be a severe test, with newspapers eager to report on cases.

Another consideration was whether there was clear membership of a church known to have a consistent stand:

> "If he belonged to a church which had a long history of pacifist doctrines as, for instance, the Christadelphians, members put more emphasis on the length of membership than on what the applicant believed, since it was obvious that (a sincere member) would accept implicitly the teaching of that Church."

RACHEL BARKER, *Conscience, Government and War*, page 33

Brethren being represented by Brother John Carter at a Tribunal in Birmingham, July 1939

Whilst this mistakenly labels us as pacifists, it does draw attention to the importance of consistency.

The verdicts open to the tribunals were similar to those of World War I. Complete or unconditional exemption meant that no restrictions were put on the applicant at all. This was relatively uncommon, and some tribunals appeared to refuse even to consider it. Those in the South and North Midlands and Northern Scotland gave no unconditional exemptions at all up to 1943, and the overall total of cases given this verdict dropped from 14% in 1939 to 5% in 1940 and 2% in 1941.

The most common verdict was exemption conditional on the applicant doing work "of National Importance", that is, work which would help to maintain the country during the wartime crisis. One common consequence of this work was being sent to another part of the country, although those who were in "reserved occupations" such as certain industrial occupations, doctors and medical staff, and teachers were exempted and allowed to stay in their jobs.

Finally, applicants could be directed to non-combatant service under military discipline, or have their application refused altogether. However, as in World War I, there was provision for appeal.

Some non-Christadelphian objectors felt so strongly about their faith that they refused even to register. As a result some 6,000 were imprisoned.

Christadelphians before the Tribunals

For the most part brethren who appeared before the Tribunals seem to have been fairly treated, and to have experienced less outright hostility from Tribunal members than brethren in the First World War. The experience of an earlier generation and the consistency of the Christadelphian stand were both important in easing the plight of brethren facing Tribunals. So too, we must believe, were the prayers of many not directly affected by conscription.

Each brother had to submit an application for exemption in writing, setting out the basis of his request for exemption. One such application is printed on pages 64-66.

THE SECOND WORLD WAR

The Military Service Committee compiled a register of all who might be affected by conscription, and made considerable efforts to ensure that every potential objector was advised about what to do. A form of words was suggested for the initial application form, and two copies of a booklet of evidence (see page 81) about the consistency of the Christadelphian stand were sent to each objector, one for his own use and the other for enclosing with his application. Each Recording Brother was also asked to sign a certificate of membership for the applicant. The Committee also suggested that each objector should be accompanied by another brother from his ecclesia, and that objectors should apply for conditional rather than unconditional exemption, but should

Certificates of Membership were issued by Recording Brethren

make quite clear their rejection of non-combatant duties under military control. Similar arrangements were put in hand by the Suffolk Street and other Fellowships of the time.

One brother found another aspect of the work of the Committee very helpful, namely, the holding of a rally for all brethren affected by the Military Service Act. This took place in London in early October 1939, chaired by Brother

THE CAPTIVE CONSCIENCE

Hubert Craddock and also involving Brethren F. W. Turner and B. R. Walker, who were to answer questions from the brethren on behalf of the Committee.

A leaflet advertising the rally is reproduced here, and *The Christadelphian* (1939, pages 514/5) reported the meeting as follows:

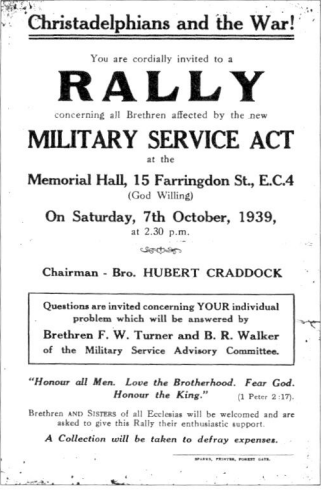

"A large company of brethren and sisters from London and surrounding ecclesias gathered in the Memorial Hall, London, EC4, on Saturday, October 7th.

The chairman, brother H. W. Craddock (Croydon), in opening the meeting, explained that the gathering was intended primarily to strengthen the sense of brotherly association among those immediately affected by the Military Service Act; but also to give brethren and sisters an opportunity of hearing at first hand what was being done on their behalf.

Brother F. W. Turner (Brixton) reviewed the work of the present Committee since its inception in 1935. He mentioned that much of what he had to say had already appeared in the circulars issued from time to time, but now there was an opportunity for the whole story to be told (as far as it was prudent to do so publicly). The re-election to Parliament of a man sympathetic to our cause, and who had actually spoken on our behalf in the House of Commons during the last war, was providential. He had shown himself thoroughly familiar with our position, and his advice and help had been invaluable. Before the Conscription Act had been discussed, our position had been made clear to the Government in the Committee's letter to the Prime Minister, which letter had been acknowledged and filed for reference. Brother Turner described the procedure adopted by the authorities in dealing with Conscientious Objectors, and read a circular letter that was sent to every brother on the Military Service Register as he became liable to be called up. This letter explained the method of claiming exemption, gave full instructions on how to complete the necessary application form, and gave advice on how to act when appearing before the Tribunal. Copies of the evidence of the genuineness of our case, as a body, were included. It was most essential that brethren should act in strict accord with the advice given; and Recording Brethren were asked to take the greatest care that Membership Certificates were

THE SECOND WORLD WAR

only given to *bona fide* Christadelphians, as upon this depended our whole standing with the authorities. In conclusion, the speaker reminded us that we had been mercifully accorded a legal right of exemption and that we should remember this fact—together with our rulers who had granted us this freedom—in our prayers.

Brother F. E. Mitchell (Tooting) and brother B. R. Walker (Brixton), then dealt ably with a large number of questions. These covered a wide field, arising out of the present circumstances, and included several dealing with the voluntary undertaking of work of national importance by brethren and sisters.

Brother R. Overton (Rugby) brought the meeting to a conclusion with a few words of an uplifting and faith strengthening character upon the theme, 'Stand still, and see the salvation of our God'."

Adverse Comments

The efficient and well co-ordinated approach of the Committee sometimes also led to adverse comments by judges, and has led a modern historian to comment:

> "Members' suspicions that Christadelphians had limited understanding of their church's teaching were partially substantiated by the fact that many applicants appeared in the Tribunal with standard statements from which they read."
>
> BARKER, op. cit., page 33

Objectors were often vigorously cross-examined by Tribunal members who, by dint of much experience, were able to ask many difficult questions relating to the understanding of specific Bible passages. This highlighted the need for every brother or sister facing a Tribunal to be able to answer for him or herself. *There is no substitute for sincere personal conviction in such circumstances.*

FIFTY QUESTIONS ASKED BY TRIBUNALS

During Tribunals of the Second World War a great many different questions were asked. These were carefully noted by the brethren attending the Tribunals in support of young Christadelphians. The following questions are selected from these records.

Section 1: Concerning membership of ecclesias

1. How long have you been a Christadelphian?
2. Why did you join the Christadelphian church? Is not your recent acceptance of the tenets of this sect the result of your desire to escape your obligation to your country?

THE CAPTIVE CONSCIENCE

3. Did your parents or friends influence you in becoming a Christadelphian?
4. Which ecclesia do you regularly attend? Can you produce a record of your attendances?
5. What active part do you take in the church apart from attending services? How much of your time do you give to this work?
6. Is it a condition of membership of your church, or is it a matter of conscience, that you object to military service? Why do you refuse to put on uniform or accept military orders?

Section 2: Unbaptized youngsters

7. If you are not a member of the Christadelphian church, why are you applying for exemption?
8. How did you arrive at your views?
9. How long have you been associated with the Christadelphians? In what way do you associate with the Christadelphians? How frequently do you attend their services?
10. How can we be sure your application is genuine?
11. Why have you not joined the Christadelphians?

Section 3: Questions based on the Bible

12. Do you read the Bible regularly? What parts of it?
13. Give 6 clear statements from the Bible which convince you that you are right in claiming exemption.
14. Do you know that the commandment, "Thou shalt not kill" refers to private murder and not to war? On occasions God expected Israel to fight. Please explain.
15. How do you reconcile your objection with David slaying Goliath?
16. Do you accept the teaching of Jesus Christ? Then please explain:

"He that hath no sword, let him buy one."
"Render to Caesar the things that are Caesar's."
"If my kingdom were of this world, then would my servants fight."
"I came not to send peace, but a sword."
The teaching of Jesus that his followers will slay the wicked.
The use of force by Jesus against the money-changers in the Temple.

17. How do you account for the verse which says, *"and there was war in heaven"* (Revelation 12:7)?
18. Do you know that civil disobedience is expressly forbidden in the New Testament?
19. How do you explain the fact that in the New Testament soldiers were allowed to become Christians, e.g. Cornelius? the Philippian jailer?

THE SECOND WORLD WAR

20. Paul said *"Fight the good fight"*. Why will you not do this?
21. Did not Peter put Ananias and Sapphira to death?
22. In loving your enemies are you not forgetting your neighbour?

Section 4: Questions related to personal conduct

23. If you saw a drunken man beating your small child, wife, father, or mother to death what would you do? Would you allow them to be killed in order to preserve your conscience?
24. Would you stand aside and watch exhibitions of brutality against Jews such as have been said to have occurred recently in Germany?
25. What would be your attitude if the country were invaded?
26. If an armed parachutist landed near you what would you do?
27. If God directed you to defend your country, would you obey?
28. Is it not your duty to assist in a war against an aggressor who advocates that Might is Right?
29. Should we surrender to Germany and Italy?
30. If a bomb dropped here, would you assist anyone who was hurt? Why then will you not join the Royal Army Medical Corps or the Air Raid Patrols? Would you join the Red Cross?
31. How can ambulance work be right under civilian control and wrong under military control?
32. If you are willing to pay taxes to support the Army, why will you not fight?
33. Do you think you have a right to food brought into this country by men who have risked their lives transporting it?

Section 5: The Christian, politics and the law

34. How do you reconcile your enjoying the privileges of British citizenship with your refusal to accept the conditions of that citizenship?
35. Are you a pacifist? Do you belong to a society which supports disarmament?
36. Has your member of parliament helped you? Do you vote? Would you join a political party?
37. Do you belong to a Trade Union? Do you pay the political levy?
38. Would you support the war financially by investing in a War Loan?
39. Do you not recognise that to enforce orderly conduct, force and the death penalty are necessary?

Section 6: Employment

40. What is your employment?
41. Do you consider your employment consistent with your conscientious objection? Is it not inconsistent to work in the production of munitions?

THE CAPTIVE CONSCIENCE

42. In choosing employment what do you regard as most important—financial reward, satisfying conscience, or future prospects?
43. What sacrifice are you making for your conscience in your job?
44. If you were granted exemption, what type of work would you be prepared to accept?
45. Are you willing to serve in the Royal Veterinary Corps? the Merchant Navy? the Medical Corps? as a special constable?
46. Christ healed the sick. Would you refuse to do non-combatant service in a military hospital?
47. Would you agree to do work which would release another man to fight?
48. Would you be prepared to work on the railways? What about trains carrying weapons or troops?
49. Is it permissible to supply food to the wounded but not bandages?
50. Do you think it is right to take office, e.g. Civil Service, under the Crown?

The wide range of questions suggests that preparation of model answers in such a circumstance may not be wholly appropriate. On the other hand it is vital that we be able to give answers based on sincerity and a full understanding of our position. Some of the above require careful consideration!

Above all, as far as is humanly possible for fallible men and women, our commitment and the conduct of our lives must adorn the gospel we seek to preach.

A BROTHER APPLIES FOR EXEMPTION

The following material provides an example of an application for exemption. The applicant used a form of words already agreed among us as representing the Scriptural reasons for our position:

"I am a Christadelphian, which is a distinctive name adopted by a body of believers in America, who in the Civil War of 1861-5 petitioned the Federal Government for and obtained exemption from Military Service on the ground of conscientious objection based on the Bible. 'Christadelphian' is the Greek form of the words, 'Brother of Christ'.

The distinctive position of the Christadelphian is:

TOWARD GOD: Separated by covenant relationship with Him (Hebrews 12:24) —

('And to Jesus the mediator of the new covenant, and to the blood of sprinkling, that speaketh better things than that of Abel');

THE SECOND WORLD WAR

and as 'bought with a price' and His 'bondservants', under obligation to render unqualified obedience to Him alone (1 Corinthians 7:23)—

('Ye are bought with a price; be not ye the servants of men');

commanded not to do violence nor kill (Matthew 26:52)—

('Then said Jesus unto him (Peter), Put up again thy sword into his place: for all they that take the sword shall perish with the sword');

nor to take vengeance (Romans 12:19)—

('Dearly beloved, avenge not yourselves, but rather give place unto wrath: for it is written, Vengeance is mine; I will repay, saith the Lord');

nor to render evil for evil (1 Thessalonians 5:15)—

('See that none render evil for evil unto any man; but ever follow that which is good, both among yourselves, and to all men').

As *'strangers and pilgrims'* to be separate from the world though living in it (John 17:11-14)—

('And now I am no more in the world, but these are in the world, and I come to thee. Holy Father, keep through thine own name those whom thou hast given me, that they may be one, as we are. While I was with them in the world, I kept them in thy name: those that thou gavest me I have kept, and none of them is lost, but the son of perdition; that the scripture might be fulfilled. And now come I to thee; and these things I speak in the world, that they might have my joy fulfilled in themselves. I have given them thy word; and the world hath hated them, because they are not of the world, even as I am not of the world');

hence to have no part in the world's politics.

TOWARD THE STATE: By divine command, to honour the King (1 Peter 2:17)—

('Honour all men. Love the brotherhood. Fear God. Honour the king');

to be in subjection to rulers and magistrates (Romans 13:1; Titus 3:1)—

('Let every soul be subject unto the higher powers. For there is no power but of God: the powers that be are ordained of God')

('Put them in mind to be subject to principalities and powers, to obey magistrates, to be ready to every good work');

and yield obedience to the laws of the realm (when not in conflict with the laws of God); rendering to all their dues (Romans 13:3-7)—

('For rulers are not a terror to good works, but to the evil. Wilt thou then not be afraid of the power? do that which is good, and

thou shalt have praise of the same: for he is the minister of God to thee for good. But if thou do that which is evil, be afraid; for he beareth not the sword in vain: for he is the minister of God, a revenger to execute wrath upon him that doeth evil. Wherefore ye must needs be subject, not only for wrath, but also for conscience sake. For for this cause pay ye tribute also: for they are God's ministers, attending continually upon this very thing. Render therefore to all their dues: tribute to whom tribute is due; custom to whom custom; fear to whom fear; honour to whom honour').

The consistent attitude of the Christadelphians is evidenced by their printed literature during the last seventy years, and by the preparation of Petitions to Parliament in 1878, 1903 and 1914, culminating in the last war in the recognition by the Authorities of their distinctive conscientious objection and the issuing to them, as Christadelphians, of the Army Council Certificates of exemption from every form of service in the forces of the State. Membership of the body of Christadelphians is only by baptism after investigation into the applicant's understanding of first principles of Bible teaching, including that set out above as their attitude toward God and to the State. Disfellowship follows any departure therefrom. On these grounds I beg to make application for total exemption from every form of service in the forces of the State.—DERRICK BANYARD"

Judges' Comments on the Christadelphian stand[1]

In the tribunal records and newspaper reports of the time there are many references to cases involving young brethren, and judges presiding over tribunals often commented on the merits of the case put to the tribunal.

The value of the consistency of the Christadelphian stand was shown by comments by Judge Stewart at the North Eastern Division Tribunal. It was reported as follows in a local newspaper:

"The comment that pacifism was no new tenet of the Christadelphian religion was made by Judge Stewart yesterday ... Where a man was a genuine and sincere Christadelphian, they were dealing with a man of a religion one of whose tenets was pacifism. That tenet ... dated back to the 1840s ..."

This comment reflects well on our consistency, even if the judge did not appreciate the difference between ourselves and pacifists. A little less comfortable was his conclusion that

"These people are not unpatriotic. That is the last thing they would want ..."

THE SECOND WORLD WAR

since this view suggests that Judge Stewart had not entirely understood the stress often laid by brethren on their pre-eminent citizenship of "another country"; that is, that although the country of their birth was Britain, their true allegiance was to God's Kingdom to come.

Other judges appreciated this point; Judge Wethered, who had seen some 170 Christadelphian objectors in the South West Tribunal, was reported as having a certain respect for Second Adventists,

> *"since none of them claimed a total right of citizenship* (author's emphasis) and were therefore logical in their objection to fighting for a country towards which they felt no particular loyalty."

Others were less sympathetic, Judge Hargreaves of the London Tribunal commenting on one occasion that the first pacifist was Pontius Pilate because he did not resist the evil demand of the Jews for Christ's crucifixion! Such a patently silly line of argument was not difficult to confute, and he still allowed Brother Dennis Adey's application for conditional exemption in 1939.

Less sympathetic still was Judge Richardson at the Newcastle tribunal who commented:

> "Middlesbrough seems one of the centres of this poisonous body,"

refusing at least one brother's application for exemption early in the war. However, the Judge's attitude was roundly condemned in the Press, which tended to sympathise with any objector treated unfairly and acted as a brake on unreasonable comments. Another judge's comment that,

> "We will call you the new contemptibles ... The room will be pleasanter when you have left it",

led to widespread condemnation.

One other comment of 1939 is worth recalling. Judge Longson of the Midlands Tribunal criticised

> "the organised coaching of young men appearing before tribunals ... I am not saying that in Birmingham there has been resort to the contemptible trickery of mock tribunals which has appeared in some other areas, but ... we have noticed organised coaching here to an extent that did not prevail at the other towns we have visited."

This comment can be viewed in two ways: on the one hand testifying to the care taken by Birmingham ecclesias to prepare young brethren, and on the other raising questions as to the wisdom of mock tribunals as a means of preparation. Whilst a consistent stand may strengthen the conscientious objector's position, answers learned but not entirely understood may weaken it. A brother who went through the experience of the Tribunals comments:

> "The answers have to come from the heart as a result of regular attention to prayer and reading. Ecclesias and parents, where possible, should ... engender in the young mind that we are in the world, not of it."

After the Tribunals

The vast majority of brethren applying for exemption were successful, conditional upon them undertaking work of National Importance.

The largest group of workers in this situation were those given land work. My own father, who had previously worked in a bank, found himself alongside Brother Ernest Foster in the employ of the Buckinghamshire War Agricultural Committee. He afterwards recounted how they found themselves for some time working with Italian prisoners of war, who might easily have overpowered them, using their spades and forks as weapons!

Not all farmers would take conscientious objectors as labourers, although as the shortage of men to work the land became more acute this resistance tended to disappear. By February 1941 86% of those sent to work on the land had found jobs, and by 1944 some 8,000 conscientious objectors were working on the land.

Farm work was no picnic for brethren unaccustomed to the heavy labour involved. Hours were long—often from dawn until dusk—and brethren found that they were often given unpleasant jobs, and sometimes put in dangerous situations. Weekend work was common, and time allowed to cycle to the nearest meeting, which might be twelve miles each way, had to be fitted in between farm duties. Older workers, some of whom had fought in the First World War, were often initially hostile. One brother was sacked after three weeks at his first farming job because of this. But few brethren who worked on the land seem to have regretted it afterwards, even though the pay was sometimes very low.

THE SECOND WORLD WAR

Brother Len Richardson was even offered the opportunity to take over the farm from a farmer for whom he worked!

Work in Hospitals and Mines

Other brethren went into medical service in hospitals, often fulfilling quite lowly roles as porters, whilst others late in the war and after were directed down the mines.

Some brethren were directed to remain in their current occupations, although this could have its problems as some employers, especially town councils, resolved not to employ conscientious objectors. Nineteen out of the sixty-three County Councils dismissed all objectors, teachers being especially singled out as a dangerous influence. However, the Government disapproved of such attitudes and actions.

WORKING ON THE LAND—A BROTHER'S EXPERIENCE

During the war brethren had many varied experiences. What follows is fairly typical of work on the land:

"When the war broke out I was the recording brother of an ecclesia in eastern England. Having to take a stand against military service in a family with a strong military tradition, I left home and went to look for work on the land.

The couple for whom I worked had been conscientious objectors in World War I and had suffered considerably. They needed help on their land but could not pay much, so I worked for them for ten shillings (50 pence) per week plus my keep. I registered as a conscientious objector and duly appeared before a tribunal, where my exemption was granted on condition I remained on the land.

I had to collect milk from farms and so was in frequent contact with a variety of people, many of whom had sons fighting and dying. Their attitudes varied: some were friendly and would ask me in for a cup of tea; a few were antagonistic. Sometimes it was possible to talk to them about how the return of Jesus would bring to an end suffering and pain.

Working on the land meant long hours in all weathers, mostly in the open air. Weariness and limited leisure made it difficult to do ecclesial work, but only two brethren in my meeting were free for Sunday duties, so we had to speak on mornings and evenings on alternate Sundays. Preparation often had to be done in the early hours of the morning!

When the vehicles went wrong, bicycles had to be used. In the winter this meant riding a trade cycle loaded with a full milk churn or up to 300 milk bottles on ice and snow. At least it meant that I was never accused of seeking an easy life!

Later I moved on to another farm and worked with a team of experienced farm hands. Keeping up at harvest time was hard work. When I was loading a farm wagon with straw one day, the cart horse set off unexpectedly and over the corner of the straw stack, catapulting me off the top onto the ground, where I landed in a heap with a broken wrist. My farming days were over and after a period of recuperation I was declared unfit for heavy manual labour by a doctor, and became a clerk in a dairy office."

Conscientious Objectors in the Armed Forces

Those developing a conscientious objection whilst in the Armed Forces faced a potentially more difficult time in persuading the authorities that they should be given exemption from further service, although after May 1940 this category of objection was recognised. However, those who applied for exemption were still court-martialled and imprisoned for three months, after which they could apply to the Advisory Tribunal, which was simply the Appeals Tribunal under another name, for release from the Forces. By 1946 some 415 had taken this route, including several who had become Christadelphians.

Brother Frank Birch came from a family which had prided itself in providing soldiers and sailors in both the wars. He had been a regular soldier in the territorial army. His decision to ask for baptism in 1942 was not easy in such circumstances, although many of his immediate colleagues and officers treated him with great consideration.

On refusing an order to accept the keys of a new transport, he was put under close arrest. The evening before his court-martial one of the witnesses came to ask him what he should say! On the following day he was sentenced to 93 days, and began his sentence in Dorchester prison. Despite warnings from the Chief Warder about the possible reactions of other prisoners, there was no hostility. From there he was transferred to Wandsworth, a dirty prison, full of professional criminals, with executions taking place at regular intervals.

Brother Percy Woodcock from Sheffield attended to represent him at the Appeals Tribunal, which he recalls as having been very helpful except for the Trade Union representative. Whilst awaiting the findings he was collected by

THE SECOND WORLD WAR

NCOs and taken to Woolwich Arsenal, where he was first locked up and then, apparently because no-one knew what to do with him, posted to the battery. When he refused this duty, he applied for and was given leave, although as soon as he got back to Sheffield a telegram ordered his return with civilian clothes. Discharged, he was sent on to the land for five years, suffering, with many other brethren, separation from home and family life in a War Agricultural Hostel.

Another brother had been brought up by Christadelphian parents, but nonetheless entered the Army, experiencing at first hand the German attack on Belgium and France in 1940 before being evacuated at Dunkirk. Back in England he began to attend the meetings again and in August 1942 was baptized.

To the Recording Brother :

Will you please bring this circular to the notice of all the members of your ecclesia.

CONFIDENTIAL.

Christadelphian Military Service Committee

21, Hendon Road,
Sparkhill,
Birmingham, 11.
May 13*th*, 1941.

Dear Brethren and Sisters,

NATIONAL SERVICE ACT, 1941.

The National Service Bill, mentioned in the recent circular issued by the Military Service Committee, has now become law. Its most important provision from our point of view is the power which it confers upon the Authorities to enrol conscientious objectors in the civil defence services, including the police reserve.

February 18*th*, 1942.

HOME GUARD.

The Government have now published the Regulations governing compulsory enrolment in the Home Guard. These will apply only in areas where an insufficient number of Home Guards is available under the voluntary system of recruitment. The requirements will depend upon military considerations and the areas and the numbers will be determined jointly by the Army Council and the Minister of Labour and National Service. It is proposed at the outset to exercise powers of compulsory enrolment only on

---

22*nd October*, 1942.

GOVERNMENT INVASION PLANS

Enquiries have been addressed to the Committee concerning the position of brethren and sisters in the event of invasion, and the following advice is offered.

It may be that invasion will never occur, but, if it does, any of us may find himself (or herself) in circumstances in which he has to think and act for himself.

Extracts of various circulars to ecclesias issued by the Military Service Committee in 1941/2

THE CAPTIVE CONSCIENCE

His officers were outraged, although many of his fellow-soldiers wished him well. Court-martial and time in a military prison followed, and failure to obey military orders there led to three days solitary confinement with bread and water. During the three days staff sergeants would kick the door and shout abuse and threats. After a day's break, the punishment was repeated; only on the third occasion did the Colonel in charge offer a further court-martial. This brother then served 112 days in Barlinnie Prison before being discharged. Even then, news of his discharge met a hostile reception from those neighbours who had lost sons in action, and eventually he moved to take up civilian work in the New Forest alongside other conscientious objectors.

The Question of Civil Defence

The impact of the war was not restricted to young men called up to serve in the Forces. As the War went on, civilians became increasingly involved.

This was not altogether unexpected. In the late 1930s the dangers of a War which would put civilians in the front line had become increasingly apparent. The bombing of Guernica during the Spanish Civil War struck terror into the hearts of many people, so that one of the earliest civil

> 26*th March*, 1942.
>
> To the Recording Brother:
>
> Dear brother, CIVIL DEFENCE.
>
> At a meeting of Area Representatives held in Birmingham on 1st November, 1941, the Military Service Committee were requested to approach the Government with a view to securing alternatives to Civil Defence for brethren liable for enrolment under the National Service Act 1941, and who conscientiously object to such service.

A Military Service Committee circular on Civil Defence

defence schemes was the setting up of Air Raid Patrols, or ARP squads as these were known. The Military Service Committee advised brethren and sisters not to volunteer for this or other civil defence schemes, because of the expectation that they would be under military or police control.

Faced with the devastation caused by the bombing of British cities, the National Government introduced the National Service Act in 1941. This Act introduced wider notions of civil defence, which now included ARP work, messenger services, rescue services, report and control centres,

THE SECOND WORLD WAR

first aid parties and the ambulance service, decontamination squads, the National Firefighting Service (which the Government described as part of a "military operation") and firewatching, which involved smothering incendiary bombs and putting out fires.

This issue of what part, if any, brethren and sisters should play in Civil Defence became a very difficult one, especially as there was no provision for conscientious objection to this service. Some brethren and sisters felt that almost any voluntary work short of actual bearing of arms was acceptable, whilst others felt that the issue was one of loyalties.

The Military Service Committee's view in 1941 was that there should be no Christadelphian conscientious objection to civil defence work, except the Police War Reserve once it became compulsory. This was based on the view that civil defence was civilian work under civilian control. It also reflected the pre-war offer that: "We are willing as a matter of duty that our powers should be used for the good of the country."

Brother Viner Hall, who was a member of a minority Christadelphian group by this time, challenged this view very strongly. He argued that the Civil Defence forces were virtually under military control, and that brethren and sisters should refuse to accept compulsory fire-watching and other similar duties.

A small group of brethren who also had this view set up "The Christadelphian Civil Defence Committee." A pamphlet published by them in January 1942 stated:

> "Civil Defence ... constitutes an insidious attack on our unique position as 'strangers and sojourners' ... National in character, it protects the life and property of Gentile states ... It is a patriotic force framed to frustrate the attacks of another state ... We must cease to be British and learn to become children of Zion. We have to renounce our earthly citizenship and transfer our allegiance and patriotism to Christ ... The incongruity of praying for the destruction of (the powers of this world), as we do when we pray 'Thy Kingdom come', while being enrolled for its defence and preservation, will be evident upon a clear understanding of the irreconcilable nature of the two citizenships."
>
> *Our Citizenship*, January 1942

THE CAPTIVE CONSCIENCE

This argument, based as it is on the Scriptural injunction to be prepared to suffer with our Lord without the camp, is one we do well to consider carefully. On the other hand, perhaps there is a lesson in Jeremiah's instruction to the exiles in Babylon: *"Seek the welfare of the city where I have sent you into exile, and pray to the* LORD *on its behalf, for in its welfare you will find your welfare"* (Jeremiah 29:7, RSV).

The question has to be asked as to whether there is any essential difference between being ready to help pull a neighbour out of the rubble of a burning building, and being part of an organised group with training to rescue people from bombed buildings, but not under military control. Where does loving our neighbour end and compromising our citizenship begin?

The majority felt that this was a matter for individual conscience. Whilst at least one member of the aforementioned Civil Defence Committee went to prison rather than compromise his stand, many brethren did do fire-watching duties. Brother Len Richardson later wrote:

> "Like the majority of members I found it difficult to see that I could be doing wrong in such a simple service of goodwill to our fellows, in trying to mitigate the loss of life and property which the bombings were causing. But as a safeguard ... I wrote a letter explaining that I was a registered conscientious objector and would be willing to undertake fire-watching duties ... so long as it was understood that I would not be prepared to come under military orders ..." *Sixty Years a Christadelphian*, page 17

In response Brother Len received an assurance that his position would not be jeopardised, which illustrates the importance of making our position clear at the outset.

Industrial Conscription and the Position of Sisters

The need felt by the authorities to involve the whole nation in the War effort led to the involvement of sisters as well as brethren.

Early in the War the government took powers which allowed it to direct civilians into war-related work. The Central Bureau of Conscientious Objectors, a non-religious body set up in the 1930s to oppose conscription, objected strongly to the absence of any conscience clause related to

THE SECOND WORLD WAR

this work, since this might have led to enforced involvement in such areas as munitions work. In the event an Appeals Board was set up, and no conscientious objectors were then directed to munitions work.

At the end of 1941, single women aged 19-31 were also made eligible for call-up, but were given the option of Civil Defence or work in industry. Sister Ruth Arnott was directed in 1942 to join the National Fire Service. Refusing on grounds of the oath to the Crown which was required, she appeared before the Appeals Tribunal in October 1942 and was directed to do fire-prevention duties in addition to the voluntary work she already undertook at a local hospital.

Dear Brethren and Sisters,

COMPULSORY REGISTRATION OF WOMEN.

Under the Government's Registration Employment Order, women born in the year 1920 are required to attend for registration on 19th April at the times and places shortly to be announced. Women born in the year 1921 will also be required to register soon after that date. The object of the registration is to ascertain the number of women who are not following any employment and also the number of women who are employed in non-essential industries with a view to their transfer to essential work. The aim of the Government is greatly to increase the number of women in war services and in munition making. The registration will apply to both married and single women, and older age groups will be required to register from time to time.

A circular alerting Sisters to the need to register

She was also directed to work of national importance, and so had to leave the solicitor's office where she worked, and work in the office of a War Agricultural Committee drainage-manager.

Where employers insisted that their female staff were essential as male staff were called up, sisters were still required to do extra work of national importance. This included hospital work, firewatching, and ambulance work. Those who received papers directing them to other occupations were interviewed at the local Labour Exchange and asked what they were prepared to do. Sister Ruby Whiteside accompanied many of the Birmingham sisters, and helped them to state their objections to such work as munitions or the women's armed forces. Some were directed to land work, whilst others went to hospital work. Perhaps the least pleasant job was to be directed to work as conductresses on the buses, but in Birmingham the young brethren arranged a rota to escort young sisters home from their work late at night. The impact of this experience on the working life of young sisters was considerable, especially since late in the war this direction of labour was extended to married women.

The Beginnings of Christadelphian Youth Circles

Another measure introduced in 1941 was the Registration of Boys and Girls Order. This encouraged young people to get involved in youth activities designed to assist the war effort. Leaflets suggested that:

> "You (the young people) are anxious to do what you can for your country at this time... (and) to do your duty as citizens and assist the present national effort."

At the same time young people below the age either of registration or of conscription were affected by the setting up of army, air force and navy cadet-corps in schools.

Such developments caused great concern to Christadelphian parents. Some brethren and sisters felt that these Government-backed measures should be resisted at all costs, since they were once again attempts by the state to coerce into conformity.

Other ecclesias decided to set up these Youth Circles for children from Christadelphian families, with a view to pre-empting any possibility of their compulsion into less acceptable groups. A membership form, the CYC promise, and a strict register of attendance, were introduced to underline the bona fide nature of the group. CYC activities included home nursing, first aid and non-military physical exercises as well as Bible study.

OBJECTS

1. To aid boys and girls to grow into the knowledge, love and obedience of Christ.
2. To provide means whereby boys or girls may associate under wise leadership for study, useful and instructive training and recreation, so moulding these activities as to promote the end in view.
3. To provide a sound basis for all activities by setting a moral standard embodied in the following promise, to be made by each boy or girl (not being a brother or sister) after a short probation as a condition of membership :
   I PROMISE TO STRIVE
   To reverence my Creator ;
   To honour my elders ;
   To do good toward all ;
   To be clean in thought and speech ;
   To think on things that are true, gracious and pure.

Member's Name ....

Address ....

Part of the CYC Membership Card

THE SECOND WORLD WAR

A few felt that youth circles were un-Scriptural and fraught with danger because they pandered to the authorities in a way that smacked of unworthy compromise, although in fact there was no compulsion from the authorities.

Brother L. G. Sargent defended the setting up of these groups by writing:

> "Whilst the subject has been brought to a head by the Government registration of boys and girls ... the movement gives shape to the thoughts of those who for some years have felt that in modern conditions the ecclesias could no longer adequately fulfil their duty to youth by an hour's Sunday School a week."
>
> *The Christadelphian*, September 1941

Nonetheless, the issue illustrates the problem that questions which arise in wartime are sometimes unexpected and difficult to deal with.

The Impact of the War on the Community

There is little doubt that the challenge of the Second World War to the faith of brethren and sisters was considerable; but the need to stand up for the Truth was beneficial to the spiritual life of the community. Many brethren who were affected recall the stronger sense of fellowship which resulted from being a *sect spoken against*; they now look back with some nostalgia to the way in which the War clarified choices between right and wrong. Shared hardship breeds strong bonds of brotherly love.

Rural ecclesias benefited considerably from those "scattered abroad" to work on the land, and young brethren grew in ecclesial and spiritual experience. Many stayed in the areas to which they had been sent, and patterns of life were altered significantly as a result.

It was the conditions of wartime that led the Christadelphian Isolation League to start a postal Bible Class. Brother Bob Clare collected, duplicated, and distributed a weekly study for the benefit of young brethren dispersed all over the UK doing their National Service as COs, often far from an ecclesia: the service has continued to the present day.

THE CAPTIVE CONSCIENCE

Effects on Health and Careers

For some, however, the cost of conscience was considerable. A few brethren who were forced to take heavy labouring work on the land suffered lasting damage to their health. In addition to the insults of fellow-workers and the scorn of neighbours, when the war eventually ended it was very difficult for objectors to return to certain kinds of employment. For example, banks often made it clear that staff who had been objectors could not expect to receive promotion. For good or ill the careers of many brethren were changed significantly, and those who were imprisoned because of their conversion when in uniform found the time spent in prison far from comfortable.

The angel of the Lord encamps around them that fear him

A number of brethren had remarkable escapes during the war. One brother worked at a pig farm which was next to a front-line RAF base. One day the RAF garrison decided that a reinforced concrete shelter at one end of the runway should be blown up to allow the runway to be extended. Out of spite towards a despised conscientious objector, the brother was not told of this plan and was in the nearby pig-pens when the explosion showered concrete, splinters and dust all around him. When he moved, only the space where he had been standing was free from debris. Later, when firewatching on three occasions, members of the group with whom he was working were killed, although he escaped unharmed.

29th October, 1945.

POSITION OF CHRISTADELPHIANS REGISTERED AS CONSCIENTIOUS OBJECTORS

In our circular letter of September 27th, 1945, brethren and sisters were informed that the Minister of Labour and National Service had under consideration a scheme for releasing conditionally registered conscientious objectors from the conditions imposed by Tribunals. It was explained that the schemes contemplated by the Minister was analagous to the Class A scheme of release at present applicable to men and women serving with the Forces.

Brethren and sisters will be thankful to know that a Bill with the object of giving effect to such a scheme received its first reading in the House of Commons on October 26th.

Military Service Committee notice of a Parliamentary Bill to allow the release of conditionally registered COs at the end of World War II

THE SECOND WORLD WAR

Casualties

Of course, the issue of providential care is a difficult one and not all brethren and sisters were so well blessed, a number being killed in bombing raids and others losing their homes and possessions—for example, in the terrible destruction of central Coventry and other air raids. But in general it is true to say that the faith of brethren and sisters in the rightness of following God's commandments in the face of opposition from those around them was fully justified in the preservation of our community in difficult times.

A commemorative card—a "second memorial of thankfulness to God"—distributed by Birmingham Central Ecclesia in 1945 (the first was issued in 1919)

---

1. The quotations from judges are taken from tribunal and other records cited in *Conscience, Government and War* by R. Barker.

9

CONSCIENTIOUS OBJECTION AFTER THE SECOND WORLD WAR

AS at the end of the First World War, many conscientious objectors had to wait a considerable length of time before being released from their "work of national importance," especially since, unlike the period after the previous World War, conscription was continued in the guise of National Service, not ending until 1960. I can remember as a boy hearing the broadcast announcements calling young men who had reached the age of conscription to register for National Service.

As a result, the issue of conscientious objection continued to be a major one for young brethren for the rest of the 1940s and 1950s. The lot of those facing tribunals continued to be difficult in some cases. The percentage of those receiving unconditional exemption dropped from 4.7% of applicants during the War to only 2.7% in peacetime. Unreasonable questions were still asked by some tribunals; for example, a photographer was asked:

> "How do you account for being a photographer when it tells you in the Commandment: 'Thou shalt not make unto thee any graven image of any likeness of anything …'?"
>
> Another Tribunal member asked: "You object on religious grounds. Then will you tell me who is the oldest character in the Book of Genesis?" When the applicant correctly answered that it was Methuselah, the next question was: "Who was Methuselah's father?"

(Hansard Record of a Debate in Parliament, July 1953)

Young brethren sometimes found themselves turned down at their first tribunal, and on appeal. Sometimes they waited weeks between the tribunal outcome and subsequent action. One young English brother living in Scotland appeared first before an Edinburgh Tribunal and was then

AFTER THE SECOND WORLD WAR

subjected to a civil action served by the Ministry of Labour and National Service, with a hearing in Dundee's Sheriff Court. This court decided that he should be taken to a local examination centre for a medical check-up.

"Evidence (from 1860 to 1951) that Conscientious Objection to all forms of service in the Armed Forces is a Denominational Characteristic of the Christadelphians": the first edition of this booklet was issued by the London Standing Committee in 1915, and this 1951 edition was used by those facing tribunals in the 1950s; it gives a chronological account of the stand taken by Christadelphians.

> # EVIDENCE
> (FROM 1860 TO 1951)
>
> that
>
> Conscientious Objection
>
> to
>
> All Forms of Service
> in the Armed Forces
>
> is a
>
> Denominational Characteristic
>
> of the
>
> Christadelphians
>
> ———
>
> All the Works quoted from or referred to in this booklet are available

Since to acquiesce with this order would have meant a return to a military court-martial, he refused to comply and was promptly fined. Because of the publicity, he lost his job. What was worse, two years later, after he had completed a college course, the civilian proceedings were reopened and he was sentenced to six months imprisonment, starting at the notorious Barlinnie Gaol in Glasgow. Fortunately, as a first offender he was moved to Saughton Prison in Edinburgh and, with remission for good conduct, served only four months.

Even in prison there were interesting encounters with a Methodist, two Jehovah's Witnesses, and a communist, all of them conscientious objectors. Throughout his time in prison an average of six letters from brethren and sisters arrived every day, even though he was only allowed one outgoing letter per month; and the late Brother George McHaffie went every week to hold a Breaking of Bread with him.

In many other cases at this time, brethren such as the late Brother Fred Mitchell and the late Brother Gordon Ramsden assisted young brethren faced by difficult circumstances.

Civil Defence Issues

Since 1945, the issue of Civil Defence has continued to be a matter of concern to the Military Service Committee. A Government proposal in 1949 for a volunteer Civil Defence Corps, which would come under Police control in an emergency, led to the advice that brethren and sisters should not get involved. This advice was repeated in the early 1950s. In 1980 the Committee wrote to the Ministry of Defence and the Home Office, primarily to remind the UK government of our position in relation to military service, but also to note our conscientious objection to compulsory Civil Defence duties. As yet this point remains unresolved, and may yet prove an important issue before the Lord returns.

The reasons for this are not hard to discover. Most Governments reserve to themselves sweeping powers, to be used in a national emergency. The sad experience of the last fifty years has been that even non-nuclear conflicts have taken a heavy toll of civilian populations caught in the midst of warring nations or factions. In the event of a nuclear emergency it is unlikely that the old niceties of legal process could or would be maintained. We do not know at what point God will deliver His servants from the final conflict of this world. But we do know that whilst the afflictions of the righteous may be many, the LORD is able to bring us through them to His kingdom.

The Work of the Military Service Committee

Throughout the period since the Second World War, the Christadelphian Military Service Committee has continued to serve as a point of advice and information. A meeting of ecclesial delegates was held in September 1962, and the following is from a letter subsequently circulated to all ecclesias:

AFTER THE SECOND WORLD WAR

"A preliminary Statement by Bro. Mitchell was given to the meeting outlining the present position. In the course of this it was stressed particularly that (a) Ecclesial Registers should be kept strictly up to date; (b) brethren baptized after leaving the Forces should advise the Authorities immediately that they have become conscientious objectors and consequently will be unable to undertake further service, combatant or non-combatant; and (c) brethren and sisters should not in present circumstances volunteer for Civil Defence duties. Bro. Newman then explained that this meeting of delegates had been called at the instigation of the surviving members of the combined Military Service Committees of the Central and Suffolk Street fellowships ... Bro. Newman also made reference to the death of Bro. John Carter who had exerted himself so much on behalf of the brotherhood in military service matters ..."

The Military Service Committee has continued to send letters and circulars to ecclesias, or publish notices in *The Christadelphian*, updating the brotherhood on relevant developments. The following is the first paragraph of a circular issued in August 1967, a few months after the Six-Day Arab-Israeli War:

CONFIDENTIAL

CHRISTADELPHIAN MILITARY SERVICE COMMITTEE

August, 1967

To the Recording Brother.

Dear Brother,

Although the Arab-Israeli war came to such an abrupt and speedy end, the world situation remains full of menace and the major powers are watching events with much anxiety. In view of the rapidity of change many brethren and sisters have expressed concern about the position, especially as regards the military service question, and we feel that this is an appropriate time to assure the Brotherhood that developments are under constant observation and that any necessary steps will be taken as soon as the need arises. It has therefore been thought advisable to issue this circular in order to remind members of Ecclesias, especially younger members, of their responsibilities in the matter and to give information which will enable recording brethren and others appointed to deal with military service matters to advise brethren and sisters who may be faced with national service problems.

In the first place brethren and sisters and others concerned

10

CHRISTADELPHIAN CONSCIENTIOUS OBJECTORS IN OTHER LANDS

MOST of the British colonies and dominions supported the British War effort in both World Wars, by sending troops to assist the British Empire, or Commonwealth, in the hour of need. These countries were often those to which the Truth had spread most readily, since they were attractive to settlers from Britain who spoke only English. As a result, brethren in these countries also found themselves called up and had to face difficulties and hardship.

NEW ZEALAND

The experience of brethren in New Zealand has been fully documented in the book *In Defence of Our Conscience*.

In common with people in other former colonies, New Zealanders felt a strong sense of duty to Britain, but there were also more local concerns after the shock defeat of Russia by Japan in 1905. Also, volunteers had fought on the side of Britain in the South African War, and as the threat of a great European War steadily increased in the first decade of the 20th century the New Zealand Parliament acted. Although the Military Service Act passed in 1909 was not implemented until 1911, it soon began to cause problems, especially since part of the Act envisaged preparatory physical training in a Senior Cadet force.

Although there had been a petition to Parliament in 1885 modelled on that prepared in Britain, in 1911 there was no central committee to advise brethren; and different ecclesias and individuals took different views as to whether young brethren should join the Cadets. There was also concern because, although the Act allowed exemption to conscientious objectors, all those exempted were to do non-combatant duties, which as we have seen elsewhere were not acceptable to brethren.

Under the 1909 Act, by 1916 nearly half the eligible male population of New Zealand was already under arms, and the ANZAC forces had taken heavy losses, especially in the ill-fated attack on the Turkish peninsula of Gallipoli in 1915. As a result, a further Military Service Act was introduced to enforce conscription more rigorously.

As in Britain, brethren offered to take up non-military duties. A Standing Committee was set up, and soon faced difficulties when the first four brethren called up were sent to military detention for refusing to sign undertakings to do non-combatant service. When they refused to put on uniform, they were punished by being sentenced to hard labour, and threatened with being forcibly taken to the fighting in Europe. Their cases and those of many other conscientious objectors caused an outcry, and the law was changed to allow exemption for those willing to do non-military work,

Conscientious Objectors in World War II doing Forestry Work at a Detention Camp in New Zealand

provided they had been members of religious bodies opposed to military service prior to the start of the War.

The alternative work consisted of being sent to state farms set up for the purpose. With minimal facilities, and only tents for accommodation, these were scarcely very comfortable, but the brethren sent to them coped with their isolation well.

Those who had been baptized after 1914 had more problems, but the good relations between the Committee and the Government led to successful appeals for them in most cases. Only one brother had major difficulties when, ill-advisedly, he applied for exemption on public interest as well as religious grounds. He was sent to military prison

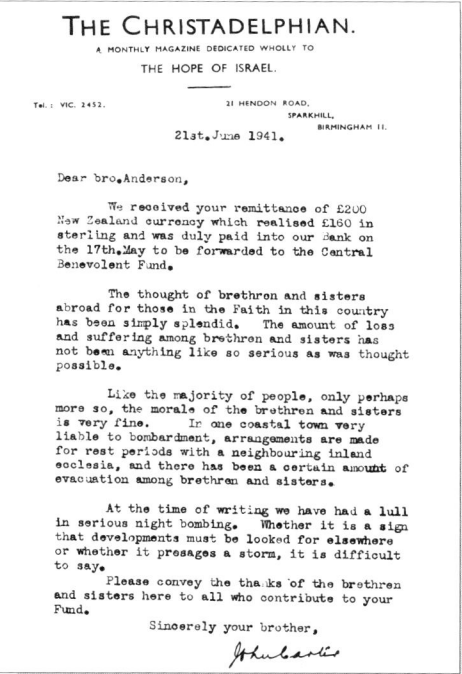

A letter to Brother William Anderson from Brother John Carter acknowledging on behalf of the Central Benevolent Fund a sum of money collected in New Zealand to help brethren and sisters in Great Britain. Shortly after this (June 1941), the New Zealand government stopped further transfers of money

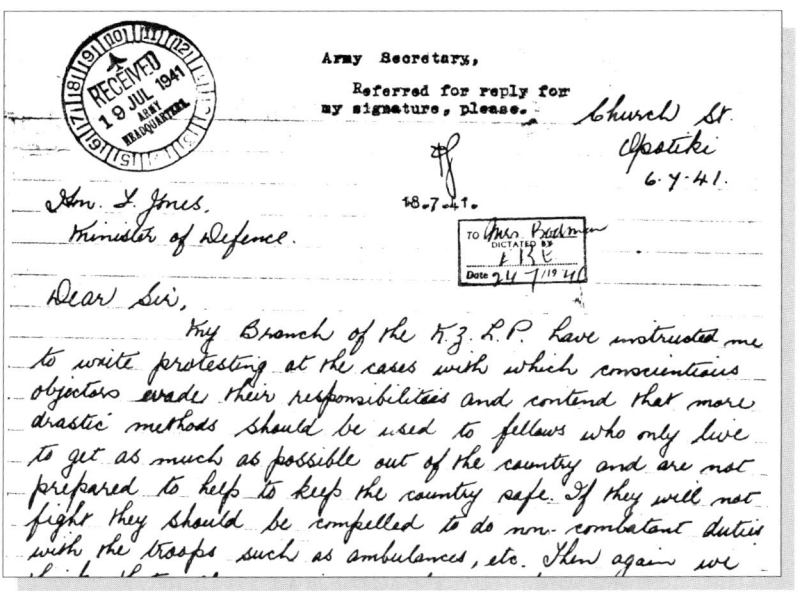

A letter (July 1941) to the New Zealand Army "protesting at the cases with which conscientious objectors evade their responsibilities ... If they will not fight they should be compelled to do non-combatant duties with the troops ..."

and then to two years' hard labour. Treated as a common criminal, on poor rations, and in inhospitable surroundings, the brother suffered considerably. He was not released until August 1919.

In the Second World War, the problems of those baptized after the War had begun were again considerable. Four newly baptized brethren had their applications and appeals rejected. There followed courts-martial, imprisonment in military prisons for three months, a further court-martial on return to Military Camp and then periods in detention camps of up to four years. Two men were converted by brethren in the camps, but sadly all four of the original detainees afterwards left the Christadelphian community.

Generally, the situation in the Second World War was better, since the Military Service Act introduced in May 1940 specified that Christadelphians and Quakers should be exempt. There was, however, some criticism of those who appeared to have come to Tribunals with pre-learned answers to questions. Many of those who were exempted were also subjected to opposition from neighbours (see letter on previous page), with graffiti on walls and gates, white feathers sent through the post, taunting of their children, and vandalism of their property. Sadly, one brother tarred and feathered was so intimidated that he left the meeting and joined up.

In one other respect the situation in New Zealand differed from that in Britain. The Standing Committee agreed to undertake civil defence work under civilian control. It was suggested that areas such as first aid, publicity, works, records, and transport were acceptable, and one ecclesia formed a voluntary aid detachment of the Red Cross.

After the Second World War conscription ended, but in 1948 it was again introduced in response to the "Cold War", lasting until 1957. Young brethren continued to have to face the tribunals, although none had any problems with exemption. A more limited scheme was also in force from 1961 to 1972, during a period when tensions were again high between the Western nations and the Communist superpowers of the Soviet Union and China.

CANADA

The experience of brethren in Canada was similar to that of those in New Zealand in many respects.

Although the position of Christadelphians had been recognised in the courts in 1917, there was no legal exemption from non-combatant service, and a number of brethren spent time in prisons and military camps in the later stages of the First World War. Three were in Kingston military prison, five at Burwash prison farm, Ontario, and two were shipped under guard to England, despite the efforts of the Standing Committee set up on the lines of the one in Britain. In all, 73 brethren were affected by conscription, 49 being given exemption, two renouncing their faith, two accepting non-combatant service, and 19 being imprisoned. Two of those imprisoned died during their imprisonment, one of influenza and the other in an asylum for the mentally ill.

IN OTHER LANDS
THE EXPERIENCES OF BROTHER JOHN EVANS

Brother John Evans was a young brother who became something of a test case in Canada. Called up in late 1917, he was refused total exemption and assigned to non-combatant service within the army. When he refused, he was arrested as absent without leave, and forcibly dressed in military uniform. As he continued to refuse orders he was put into an overseas draft and transported with common criminals to the ship to be taken to Europe. On board, he was court-martialled for refusing further orders, and sentenced to four days in the open bows of the ship pounded by the waves.

On arrival in England he was taken to a military camp, court-martialled again, and sentenced to prison. Transferred under guard to Wandsworth prison, he was housed in a cell 12 x 7 feet, under military guard, and for a time survived on punishment rations of 6 ounces of bread and water morning and evening. Because of his steadfast refusal to submit to army orders he was beaten up, pushed down a flight of stairs, and flogged with a rope.

After seven weeks on a starvation diet he was returned to the military camp and transferred to a railway corps, where his continued refusal to accept military discipline meant he ended up in military prison in the company of a murderer and other criminals. In August 1918 he was told he was being drafted to France, and an attempt was made to force him to undertake training for gas attacks by putting him in a gas-filled room.

During all this time no-one in Canada knew where Brother Evans was, not even his wife, since he was allowed no letters. However, he did manage to write to the London Standing Committee, and it may have been due to their intervention that the order drafting him to France was cancelled at the last minute. However, he was again court-martialled and, despite orders that he was to be sent back to Canada, eventually sentenced to hard labour, being paraded in front of 1,000 men, his army cap thrown in the dirt as a mark of disgrace.

The sentence started in a small cell in Pentonville prison with a bed of planks covered by a thin straw mattress. He was put to work sewing mailbags, and fed on minimal rations of porridge without milk or sugar for breakfast; on bean or barley soup for lunch; and on bread, cocoa and a small piece of fish for supper. Yet mercifully he was at last able to have a visit from Brother John Owler, who broke bread with him in his prison-cell.

Brother Evans was eventually released on the orders of the Home Secretary, and shipped back to Canada on the liner Aquitaine with other soldiers returning from the war, which by now had ended. Still held under open arrest, he was first threatened with further punishment, but then allowed leave and an honourable discharge!

In all this Brother Evans found that his steadfast stand won respect from many of his fellows, including the criminals with whom he was imprisoned; and there is little doubt that his faithfulness under extreme pressure helped to bring about the Alternative Service Act which allowed conscientious objection in the Second World War.

The experience of Brother Evans is described more fully in **Test Case for Canada,** *published in 1972 by his son, Brother E. R. Evans.*

After the First World War ended, the Standing Committee was disbanded until the threat of Fascism in Europe caused it to be reconstituted in 1934. A circular letter, sent to all brethren in early 1936, contains advice which still holds good today:

"FIRST, build up a character, based upon the Christ Law, which will be above reproach or question, as a testimony that you have truly learned of Christ, to whose law you will appeal.

SECOND, make sure and certain, by knowledge, that you understand the Scriptural grounds fully, which form the basis of your stand against civil and military service, where the oath of allegiance to any but God is involved."

(Letter of the Canadian Standing Committee dated January 1936, cited in a Summary report of the work of the Committee by Brother W. A. Weir)

The Committee, in which members from the Suffolk Street and Central fellowships worked together, also advised brethren to keep away from the manufacture of munitions. They later also advised brethren and sisters not to purchase shares in companies catering for the war effort, nor to buy war bonds.

When the Second World War commenced, the Canadians once again supported Britain, and in late 1940 conscription was introduced. The Canadian Standing Committee met with a Government Minister to make representations for exemption. Whether it was their representations or the prayers which accompanied them, the result was that Christadelphians were granted indefinite postponement of call up. Having offered to do work of National Importance, brethren had at first to work under civilian control as direct-

IN OTHER LANDS

```
-RP 7411 NLT JOHN CARTER 21 HENDONRD BHAM =

DOES YOUR STANDING COMMITTEE APPROVE MEMBER JOINING
NATIONAL FIRE SERVICE REPLY IMMEDIATELY =

                                        H JENNINGS
```

A telegram from Brother Jennings (Toronto) to Brother John Carter, seeking advice on joining the Fire Service. Brother Carter's reply telegram (followed up by a letter) read:

"INDIVIDUAL CONSCIENCE DETERMINES. ALTERNATIVE WORK USUALLY PREFERRED AND GENERALLY ALLOWED. LETTER FOLLOWING. CARTER."

ed by a local Board, and had to contribute all but $5 of their monthly wages to the Red Cross.

From 1942 this work was to be done in camps organised by the Department of Mines and Forestry. These camps were remote from the population centres of Canada, and offered only primitive accommodation, limited rations, and little warmth against the severity of the Canadian winter. There was also the uncertainty of not knowing when the call to a camp would come, with little notice given. Only two weeks' leave were allowed in twelve months, although visitors were allowed at weekends, and the brethren were able to break bread together. Tragically, the prospect of this difficult regime in the forests led to the suicide of one young brother.

The camps were finally all closed when the war ended in 1945.

THE CAPTIVE CONSCIENCE
THE EXPERIENCES OF A CANADIAN BROTHER IN WORLD WAR TWO

The following account is fairly typical of the experiences of Canadian brethren in World War Two:

In December 1942, being twenty years of age, I received my call-up papers from the Department of National Defence. I applied for exemption from military service on the grounds of conscientious objection. As a result of the hearing, I was granted exemption conditional upon working in a labour camp.

On December 20th, 1942, I took the overnight train to Sault Ste. Marie, arriving early in the morning with the temperature 30 degrees below zero. Some 25 of us were then taken by truck 100 miles to the Montreal River, suffering greatly from the cold on the way.

When we arrived, the manager of the camp made it very clear he considered us the dregs of society and traitors for not going to fight. Our ration books were taken from us, so that we received no sugar or butter. Breakfasts consisted of porridge with a little milk, dry bread and coffee; lunch, stew, dried bread and tea; for dinner we also had fried or baked potatoes, but rarely any other vegetables. Dessert was rice pudding or apple sauce.

Work was hard, building roads using picks, shovels and explosives; or foraging for wood to keep the bunk-house warm in the bitterly cold nights. Fortunately, I was given the job of driving the supply truck to and fro to Sault Ste. Marie, a job which, despite blizzards and the danger of breakdown in wilderness territory, was less demanding than some.

Despite the hardships of cold and snow and the monotonous diet, our camp was well run until April 1943, when the camp was closed and the men were sent to farms in Southern Ontario. I went to a farm outside Wallenberg, where the farmer put me to work spreading the accumulated manure from the winter. Towards the end of August I was allowed to go back to my parents' farm, and remained there until the end of the war.

AUSTRALIA

Many of the problems faced by brethren in other countries were not widely experienced by Australian ecclesias until the Second World War, although a scheme for compulsory military training was introduced in 1911.

When this was re-introduced in the Second World War, an Australian Standing Committee made the position of the

IN OTHER LANDS

community quite clear to the Government, and put forward a petition presenting the reasons for conscientious objection.

The petition, which is reproduced below, illustrates the common approaches to governments taken by ecclesias in different parts of the world. However, it is worth noting that terminology varied considerably—non-combatant service having a different connotation in Australia:

28th September, 1939

The Rt. Mon. R. G. Menzies, P.C., K.C. M.H.R.
Prime Minister of Australia,
CANBERRA A.C.T.

Sir,

I am directed by the Australian Christadelphian Standing Committee, representing the major section in Australia of the religious body known as Christadelphians, to make this petition to you in the matter of military service required under the Defence Act 1903-1939.

1. All Christadelphians are conscientiously opposed to the bearing of arms, or taking part in warfare, on the ground that the Bible, which they revere as the Word of God, commands them to refrain from killing or doing violence of any kind to their fellowmen, and, consequently, they entertain the firm conviction that they are debarred, by Divine Command, from taking part in the conflicts that arise between nations.

2. Conscientious religious objection to military service has been an article of faith of Christadelphians since the beginning of their existence as a body, over 90 years ago, as is evidenced in their literature current among them for many years, and in their Statement of Faith, which must be believed in by those who are admitted to their fellowship, and who must first satisfy responsible and specially appointed elders of their understanding and belief of Christadelphian doctrines, and submit to the ordinance of baptism (immersion) as commanded by Christ. These conditions preclude the membership being suddenly augmented by those merely desirous of evading military service.

3. Members of our body recognise and discharge the duty of submitting to the laws enacted by the Government, where those laws do not conflict with the commands of our Lord Jesus Christ and his Apostles; but where human statutes impose obligations contrary to Divine principles, which they have by a solemn covenant bound themselves to observe, they feel that they are compelled "to obey God rather than men," whatever the consequences may be.

THE CAPTIVE CONSCIENCE

4. On many occasions during the past 35 years similar representations have been made on behalf of this body to successive Governments of the Commonwealth of Australia, so that this petition is not an expedient for the present emergency.

5. Provision is made in the Commonwealth of Australia Constitution Act, Section 116, inter alia, that no law shall be made "for prohibiting the free exercise of any religion", and abstention from bearing arms or engaging in war in any capacity has always been a tenet of religion of all Christadelphians.

6. We recognise that provision is made under Section 61 (i) for exemption from military service of persons who satisfy the prescribed authority that their conscientious beliefs do not allow them to bear arms, but that such exemption shall not extend to duties of a non-combatant nature, and that under Section 143 (3) such persons shall, as far as possible, be allotted to non-combatant duties.

7. We have no objection to performing non-combatant duties as such, but enlistment in the Active Military Forces necessitates taking the oath, or affirmation, of enlistment, which requires a declaration to resist His Majesty's enemies, and, being under military control, to do combatant duties when required, which as before stated we cannot conscientiously undertake to do.

8. We realise that conditions might arise in times of national emergency demanding the aid of all, and we respectfully submit that there are many forms of national service (not under military control, and not associated with the manufacture of arms, munitions, materials for the destruction of human life and such-like) which would not be incompatible with our religious beliefs, and which our members would willingly perform when required, and so discharge their obligations to the State as far as possible.

9. We, therefore, humbly request that by an amendment of the Act, or in the promulgation of Regulations defining the powers of the "prescribed authority" referred to in Section 61 (i), provision be made for essential national service, not under military, naval or air control, and not for the manufacture of arms, munitions, materials for the destruction of human life and such-like, to be regarded as non-combatant service, to which members of the Christadelphian community could be allotted under Section 143; and that the taking of the oath or affirmation, prescribed by the Act, shall be dispensed with in such case.

10. Our sole concern is that we may be allowed to continue to carry out our sincere religious convictions, and render obedience to God as we see it, and at the same time not be in opposition to the law of the land. This is the reason we wish there should be no legal restrictions imposing obligations that, if complied with, would compromise us in our unqualified allegiance to Christ.

IN OTHER LANDS

11. Liberty to live according to our conscience is quite as vital, and in our belief is fraught with consequences as great to us individually, as those high principles of freedom and free belief to preserve which, it is claimed, the British Nation has engaged in war with Germany, as so eloquently set forth by Mr. Chamberlain, Mr. Roosevelt, and yourself, and we have every confidence that you will give full and favourable consideration to our case, as stated herein, and we trust that you will grant our petition.

Yours respectfully,

For the Australian Christadelphian Standing Committee,

A. W. BONNER,
Secretary

Despite prolonged correspondence, the Australian Government at first refused to recognise the objection to non-combatant service under military control and, for a time, those who faced magistrates or higher courts sometimes encountered difficulties, with one young brother suffering a short prison sentence. Later the courts recognised Christadelphian applications for exemption from all military service. Other brethren faced problems of employment when the companies for which they worked turned production over to munitions, especially since there were strict controls over changes of employment.

Following the Second World War, the National Service Act was passed in 1951 requiring young men to undertake six months' service followed by five years in the Reserve Forces. This was amended in 1964 to two years' training and three years as a Reservist, and continued until the compulsory elements were removed by Prime Minister Whitlam in 1973.

SOUTH AFRICA

The issue of conscientious objection first became of significance to the brethren of South Africa at the time of the Boer War, a civil war between the Afrikaner settlers, who had originally come from the Netherlands, and the British settlers and government.

Little detailed information remains of that period, but the experience of one brother demonstrates that there can be particular difficulties when a civil war brings together the issues of ethnic identity, patriotism, and military service.

THE CAPTIVE CONSCIENCE

Brother Johann Laffnie was a farmer in the Transvaal, baptized into Christ in 1892. By the time the War broke out in 1899 there was a small ecclesia meeting at his farm, including a number of members of his family. At first there was no question of him being pressed into service in the Boer army, since at the outset of the war he had been seriously ill; but when he recovered he came under intense pressure to join the Boer farmers fighting the British. His son-in-law and fellow Boer, Brother Abraham Dannhauser, seems to have come under the same pressure.

Since the war was mostly fought by Boers in irregular guerrilla commandos and with a fierce conviction that God was on their side, those Boers who refused to help on grounds of conscience must have had a difficult time. Even worse, when the British Army was mopping up the stubborn Boer resistance, they were unable to distinguish between the non-uniformed Boer irregulars and anyone who had not been involved, so rounded up all the young Boer men and imprisoned them. Brother Abraham Dannhauser was probably the brother who turned up in Durban after the war shortly after his release from imprisonment in a prisoner of war camp on the island of St. Helena, where he had spent a whole year imprisoned with Boer soldiers!

Perhaps because of the experience of the Boer War, no attempt was made to introduce conscription into South Africa during the First World War. The South African Defence Act of 1912 did set out the conditions for a general mobilisation, but a short-lived pro-German Boer uprising in 1914 made it clear that the issue of being forced to fight for the British Empire would raise great problems for the country. Although South African troops did fight against the Germans in South West Africa, and to some extent elsewhere, they were all volunteers. This was also the situation during the Second World War.

The 1912 Act had made limited provision for conscientious objectors and, when it was updated in 1957, this provision was carried forward with few changes. Whilst recognising the possibility of genuine objection, the Act allowed non-combatant service as the only alternative to full involvement in fighting units—and then only to those who were *bona fide* members of a church clearly opposed to military service.

IN OTHER LANDS

Detention

The testing time for young South African brethren came when the government introduced conscription of white young men in the early 1960s in order to help it defend apartheid against internal and external attacks. Faced with the unacceptability of non-combatant service, young brethren were subject to arrest, trial and imprisonment. A number of brethren actually served terms ranging from one to three years in prison, whilst a few left the country to avoid a similar penalty.

It is interesting to look back over the South African *Lightstand* magazines for the late 1970s and early 1980s, together with other reports in *The Christadelphian*. The ecclesias showed great solidarity with their young brethren, and month by month the news items expressed thanks on their behalf for letters received and the occasional visits that were allowed.

Brother Colin Kaiser was sentenced to detention for three years in the barracks at Voortrekkerhoogte, Pretoria. When he was released, the following were some of the comments in the August 1985 issue of *Lightstand*:

> **Pinetown.**—On Saturday, 20th July (1985), the day after Bro. Colin Kaiser's release, he joined us as we gathered in a meeting of thanksgiving to our Heavenly Father for His care and protection towards our brother during his absence, and for his safe return to us after 1096 days, during which he has stood as a reminder to us of the allegiance we owe to our God and Father.
>
> **Durban.**—We were able to join with the Pinetown Ecclesia and Bro. Colin Kaiser and his family, in the devotional service held to give praise to the Lord for Colin's safe return. We rejoice with them all and pray for Colin's continued well being.
>
> **Johannesburg.**—This month has brought the release of our Bro. Colin from detention, for which we have all been praying. We share in the joy of Bro. Colin and his family at this time.
>
> **Pietermaritzburg.**—We rejoice with Bro. Colin Kaiser and his family with being released from detention. We thank our Heavenly Father for continually being with our brother and returning him to us after 3 years.

THE CAPTIVE CONSCIENCE

A Military Service Committee had been set up in South Africa, as elsewhere, and gave valuable assistance to the brethren faced with conscription. As a result of protests from various quarters, the law was changed in 1983. Under the new law, the test became one of personal religious conviction, sincerely held in an honest and genuine conscience. The sentencing to detention was also ended, with community service substituted.

Christadelphians in South Africa were required by law to send representatives to a new Board for Religious Objection. At the first meeting of this Board at Bloemfontein in March 1984, at which Brother Anthony Oosthuizen represented the Christadelphians, the presiding judge commented favourably on the way in which Christadelphian objectors were helped by their community to get their applications properly drawn up. The first six applications were accepted without question in only ten minutes! The Anglican representative present, however, asked for a statement concerning the Christadelphian view of war to be clarified.

The reply is reprinted below:

WHY CHRISTADELPHIANS ARE NOT PACIFISTS

Draft Addendum to the *Statement of the Christadelphian Position in Relation to Military, Naval and Air Service:*

The statement in the penultimate paragraph on page 3 that: 'Christadelphians do not hold the view that, under the present constitution of the world, war, as such, is necessarily wrong' is not to be construed as permitting any liberty of conscience to individual members to involve themselves in conflicts which they may perceive to be part of the purpose of God as revealed in the Bible; nor is it in any way intended to be a contradiction of the traditional Christadelphian position outlined on pages 1 and 2. It arises from the need to distinguish the Christadelphian position from that of the pacifist, who believes that all wars everywhere are wrong and contrary to the will of God.

Christadelphians believe that war may be seen as an instrument which God, in His wisdom, uses to bring about the fulfilment of His purpose on earth. War was used in Old Testament times to destroy idolatrous nations (Deuteronomy 7:1-6; 9:1-6) and to punish the Israelites for their iniquity (2 Chronicles 36:14-21; Jeremiah 32:28-35; Luke 21:20-24). It will be used again in the future to humble

IN OTHER LANDS

Israel (Zechariah 14:1,2) and the rebellious nations of the world (Joel 3; Revelation 19:11-21).

The extent to which war is currently used by God in direct fulfilment of His purpose is impossible to determine, although it seems clear that some contemporary conflicts are in accordance with Bible prophecy, e.g. the hostility between Jew and Arab in the Middle East (Psalm 83; Ezekiel 28:24-26; 35:1-6).

Christadelphians nevertheless believe that it would be wrong for a disciple of Christ to involve himself in armed conflict in the present dispensation. The call to discipleship is an exhortation to follow the non-violent example of the Lord Jesus Christ, and the will of God as expressed in the commandments of Christ, is the ONLY standard of right and wrong for all disciples, as explained on pages 2-4 of this Statement.

If, however, at his second advent, Christ should order his disciples into battle, then, and only then, would Christadelphians take up arms in obedience to the commands of their King (Psalm 149:4-9; Revelation 2:26-27; 19:11-19).

God is working His purpose out at various different levels simultaneously, and Christadelphians see nothing incongruous in asserting that the disciple of Christ is called to serve Him in faith, at one level (1 Peter 2:21-23), while God, through the instrumentality of war and politics, continues to guide the history of mankind, at another level, to its appointed end (Daniel 2:44; Zechariah 14:9).

While Christadelphians, therefore, are not permitted to take part in war, they recognise that God may use wars to bring about His declared purpose. In this sense, then, war is not necessarily in general terms wrong, although it would be wrong for the individual disciple of Christ to participate in it.

This addendum satisfied the Board, but a number of other difficulties were subsequently encountered in relation to community service. A newsletter of 1986 refers to problems over bank loans, leave, and subsequent employment; and to the call for older men in some areas to register for commando service.

Conscription was abolished in 1993 as one of the moves towards a more democratic form of government, and the manpower requirements of the Defence Force are now met by volunteers from all racial groups. As a result, the national service problems faced by South African brethren have diminished for the time being, but given the rapid rate of political change in the country the future remains uncertain.

THE CAPTIVE CONSCIENCE
THE UNITED STATES OF AMERICA

The experience of the American Civil War contributed to a marked reluctance on the part of the United States to become involved in the First World War. However, fears of a German victory, combined with German U-boat attacks on American ships bringing supplies to Britain and her allies, led to a declaration of war against Germany in April 1917.

The brethren of the Jersey City Ecclesia had anticipated this possibility by presenting a petition to Congress drafted on the lines of the British petitions, "asking for full exemption from every form of military and naval service". A brother at the time wrote: "Now is the time for the brethren in this country to declare themselves in reference to war, so that in days to come they may be regarded in their true light, and not as those who shirk their duty". This was, and still is, wise advice.

In May 1917 the petition was presented to Congress jointly by the Amended and Unamended ecclesias and other information was prepared for brethren of military age.

With only a small army in existence, the US government at first relied on volunteers, but also passed a Selective Service Act to enlist men for future service. In all about 24 million men were registered under this scheme, with 5 million registered for military service. Some 2.5 million actually served in the Armed Forces.

Young brethren who had a conscientious objection to military service had to appear before draft boards, made up of patriotic citizens who had volunteered for the task. These Boards only had the options of granting absolute exemption, stipulating non-combatant service, or denying the request altogether. If turned down by the draft board, the applicant could appeal. Each appellant was investigated by the Federal Bureau of Investigation (FBI), and had to appear before a hearing officer appointed by the Government. If this failed, the only further appeal possible would be to the President of the country. Those who failed to report for duty were imprisoned for two years, or up to the end of the War.

IN OTHER LANDS

Local boards varied a good deal in their approach to conscientious objectors. In some areas those who belonged to churches known to be opposed to military service received exemption with little difficulty. In certain other areas, the boards refused most applications.

The experience of young brethren also varied, some being granted exemption and others denied it. In December 1917

An American Recruiting Poster (compare the Kitchener Poster on page 30)

a further joint resolution was presented to President Wilson. It reported: "Christadelphians ... have been forced against their will to enter the army camps and have been held by the military authorities. We believe that all (these) Christadelphians ... should be considered as prisoners unlawfully held by the military arm of the government."

THE CAPTIVE CONSCIENCE

As in the UK, the proposal was put forward by the ecclesias that young brethren should undertake civilian work of value. However their pleas went unheeded; in March 1918 clarification of the rules for non-combatant service only served to emphasize the lack of civilian service as an alternative and the Exemption Committee which had been set up increasingly found itself trying to help brethren forced into military surroundings.

It succeeded in keeping all but 4 of 47 brethren in military camps from being sent to prison, giving wise advice on how to present evidence of the consistency of the Christadelphian stand in general and of their own position. Eventually the lobbying of the Government helped to bring about the introduction in May 1918 of a scheme which allowed objectors to be placed on farms.

THE EXPERIENCES OF TWO BRETHREN

Brother N. S. Mowry of Worcester, Massachusetts was one of the brethren who found himself drafted into military service. On arrival at Camp Devens in October 1917 he refused to put on uniform or sign any papers until he was transferred to a segregated conscientious objectors squad. When others in the squad agreed to accept non-combatant duty, Bro. Mowry refused to accept any form of military service. On 5th November he was paraded before the entire camp hospital staff of over 40 doctors and berated for his unwillingness to accept duty as a medical orderly. When he sought to explain his position he was confronted by anger and threats. At the beginning of December the objectors were deprived of food, which led to protests to the War Department and the restoration of rations. A little later, when the War Department asked camps to identify objectors to all military service, the Commander refused to accept any would be allowed to object to non-combatant service. In May 1918 Brother Mowry and other objectors were court-martialled but action was then suspended as the war drew to an end. Eventually he was released at the end of the war.

Brother Ernest Wells of the Berea Ecclesia, Meckenburg (VA), was less well blessed. Arrested for failure to report for military duty in January 1918, he was taken to Camp Lee and given only bread and water. Charged with being a deserter, he was court-martialled and sentenced to 20 years hard labour, later reduced to 10 years. Transferred to Fort Leavenworth whilst the Exemption Committee argued for his release, he died before the end of the war.

IN OTHER LANDS

The comment was made that, generally speaking, Christadelphians "seemed to obtain a recognition that other religious societies failed to receive".

World War II

The United States also remained neutral at the start of the Second World War, entering the conflict only after the Japanese launched a surprise attack on Pearl Harbour in Hawaii in 1941. However, such was the alarm at the early successes of Germany and her allies that in September 1940 the American Congress passed the first peacetime conscription bill, and reintroduced the draft, as it was known. This law was further strengthened in 1941, and required all young men to register for military service.

As elsewhere, brethren refused to undertake non-combatant duties, since the American Government made it quite clear that the purpose of such forces was to enable the war to be carried on most effectively. Once again the Military Affairs Committee of Christadelphians gave invaluable help.

Those given exemption were required to perform alternative service, which often meant working in State mental hospitals, as forest fire-fighters, or in charitable organisations. These jobs were poorly paid; indeed, in the Civilian Public Service camps individuals or their ecclesias were required to provide $35 a month for expenses. It was usually stipulated, moreover, that the objector should be employed at least 100 miles from home. Most brethren were able to get exemption, but one or two were imprisoned. In all 127 brethren were in such alternative service.

During the subsequent "Cold War", Americans continued to be drafted into the armed forces, and it was not until 1975, at the end of the Vietnam War, that conscription ended. However, it was now easier for objectors, since those continuing in education could ask for deferment of their service. Even today, all young men reaching the age of 18 are required to register for what is known as the "standby draft." Normally there is no difficulty in registering as a conscientious objector.

THE CAPTIVE CONSCIENCE

> US GOVERNMENT COMMENT ON CHRISTADELPHIANS
>
> "The largest churches which retained doctrines of conscientious objection in World War II were the Mennonite, Brethren and Friends [Quakers]. Together with certain smaller denominations, such as the Christadelphian and Molokan, these three made up what were commonly known as the 'pacifist churches' or 'Historic Peace Churches' ... Christadelphians have consistently maintained that their faith prohibited participation in the armed forces of any country, whether in times of peace or time of war ... It should be noted that for each 1,000 members of the Christadelphian Church in 1936 there were 49.4 assignees in [alternative service] camps from 1940 to 1947 ... For other denominations the number per 1,000 was: Mennonite 40.3; Friends 9.6; Brethren 7.8; Jehovah's Witnesses 7.1; Church of God 1.2 (all others less than 1 per 1,000). It would appear that the members of the Christadelphian Church followed more closely than any other denomination the doctrine of their denomination as it related to conscientious objection and refusal to enter the armed forces."
>
> From "Conscientious Objection", published by Selective Service System, US Govt. Printing Office, 1950

OTHER COUNTRIES

Most of the older former British colonies around the world based their approach to the question of conscientious objectors on the same principles as were followed in Britain, although local practice in the application of those principles varied widely. Elsewhere in the world, however, brethren often faced difficult situations.

Guyana

During the mid 1980s it became compulsory to undertake National Service. This consisted of one year's training in civil and political matters, followed by six weeks' army training under Army control and in military uniform, including compulsory target practice with live ammunition. There was no exemption, and those who tried to refuse faced the loss of jobs and such opportunities as University places. Children also were to attend cadet-training. This put con-

IN OTHER LANDS

siderable strain on ecclesias in Guyana, which eventually decided to withdraw from anyone undertaking the military training. We can be thankful that the situation in Guyana has since eased.

El Salvador

Here brethren also faced similar problems caused by forcible recruitment by officials, a situation which has also improved in recent years.

Jamaica

In 1976, the Marxist government introduced a compulsory uniformed National Youth Service. The aim was not truly "national" at all. Its purpose was to speed up the indoctrination of youth in Marxism-Leninism. In theory, conscripts had the option of military, hospital, or agricultural service, but in fact the choice was rarely honoured. In practice, only young people who were known to be committed socialists were entrusted with weapons. No Christadelphian was forced into actual military service, and there was no oath, so for a time the presence of one or two brethren and sisters in uniform at ecclesial meetings was not unusual. The fall of the Marxist government in 1980 led to the discrediting of the National Youth Service, which was then abolished, ending this uncomfortable situation.

Germany

In only one country with which Britain and its allies have been at war, has there been an indigenous Christadelphian community, namely Germany.

In 1914 there were only 10 German brethren and sisters in Stuttgart, as a result of the work of Brother Albert Maier, who was baptized in the United States in 1885 after emigrating, and subsequently went back to Germany to try to convert some of his fellow Germans. When war broke out, Brother Ludwig Knupfer, who was about 18 at the time, was called up. Brother Maier submitted an appeal on his behalf to the military authorities, who allowed him to be a "non-combatant" air observer. Captured by the French, he spent his time as a prisoner translating part of *Christendom Astray* into German.

THE CAPTIVE CONSCIENCE

Afterwards Brother Maier and Brother Knupfer worked with others to build up ecclesias of 25 members in Stuttgart, 25 in Esslingen, and 30 in Bonn, with a few others in Berlin. By this time the Nazi regime had been established, and conscription followed as Adolf Hitler became more and more aggressive in his defiance of the other powers of Europe.

During the Second World War the brethren and sisters in Germany suffered many hardships and dangers. Breaking of Bread and other meetings were held from house to house; some escaped unscathed from the destruction of their property by bombing; others were interrogated and imprisoned; one—Brother Albert Merz—was shot for refusing the call of conscription.

THE EXPERIENCES OF BROTHER ALBERT MERZ

Brother Albert Merz was a member of the Stuttgart Ecclesia. A photo of 1934 (see opposite) shows him as part of a large gathering of brethren and sisters reported to have been visited by English brethren.

When the Second World War came, Brother Albert Merz was called up to join an infantry regiment. Because there was no right of exemption for conscientious objectors he was arrested on refusal, and taken to Berlin for trial. Strenuous efforts were made by the authorities to persuade him to accept that he must join the army. After the final hearing of his case, the defence lawyer appointed by the State also tried to persuade him to change his mind, as the letter below shows:

Erich Höhne,
Lawyer and Notary
at the Landgericht Berlin   Berlin 22. February 1941

To Rifleman Albert Merz,
at present in the Military Detention Centre, Berlin-Tegel

Yesterday's proceedings ended with the passing of the death-sentence on you. No other outcome was indeed possible since you remained deaf to all arguments. Things turned out exactly as I predicted to you during our meeting. You must yourself admit that the Presiding Judge made the most strenuous efforts to cure you of your mistaken view. The more I think about your position, the more incomprehensible your conduct becomes for me. You will remember that the Presiding Judge read out to you the text of the passage in the Bible where it says that everyone must be subject to the higher powers and that the powers that be are ordained of God. If you

IN OTHER LANDS

Brethren and sisters at Stuttgart photographed on the occasion of Brother Stanley Ramsden's visit in 1934. Brother Albert Merz is indicated with an arrow.

yourself always say that for you as a Christadelphian the Bible is the only authority, then you must take this text into account too. Yet you were not able to say a single word in answer to this passage. If an authority, such as our Führer in this case, calls upon the German people to defend themselves, if necessary by force of arms, against the intended attacks of jealous neighbouring peoples and if he, as the authority, has introduced universal military service, then this represents, in the light of the Bible passage previously mentioned, a command which is approved by God also and which every subject must obey.

However, all is not yet lost for you; although this grave sentence has been passed on you, it can still be reversed if you will allow yourself, at the eleventh hour, as it were, to be convinced of the incorrectness of the position that you have maintained so far and now declare that you are willing to perform military service without reservation.

I hope that in the face of death you will yet come to this better understanding. Your position, which you adopt so decidedly without even giving consideration to the views and ideas of your countrymen, who seek only your good and who are also good Christians, is in my eyes not at all an assertion of original Christian teaching, as you mistakenly believe. Rather, in your attitude can be heard the voice of the spirit of Antichrist, the spirit of evil, that has led you into the sin of pride, as if only you and the few adherents of your false doctrine had the correct understanding of the teaching of

THE CAPTIVE CONSCIENCE

Jesus Christ and all we others offend against the command of God. My firm conviction, however, and that of every true German is that the good Lord will take greater pleasure in a man who has given his life in the fulfilment of his duty towards his country than in someone who throws away his life fruitlessly, simply because out of pride he refuses to listen to better understanding. Such conduct can under no circumstances be pleasing to God.

As the defence counsel officially appointed by the court I have considered it my duty to urge you to consider your position one last time. Should you then come to a different conclusion, you must immediately ask to appear before the court again and make a statement accordingly. However, the matter is extremely urgent, for you have only a few days in which to do so.

Heil Hitler!

(signed)

Brother Albert remained faithful to his Lord and so was shot on Friday, April 4th, 1941 at 5.40 am in the Brandenburg prison in Berlin. Four of his family were sent to a concentration camp. To his brethren and sisters he wrote: "You will know my belief and hope. For me to live is Christ and to die is gain."

The last letters of Brother Albert Merz:

Berlin, 23.2.41

To all my dear ones,

It is hard for me to write to you today, not on my own account but because I know that this letter will cause you grief. So I beg you not to take it too hard. You all know my faith and my hope: 'For me to live is Christ and to die is gain'. So do not weep over me, even if the worst happens to me, but rather be strong and of good courage. The fact that I was condemned to death on February 21st and am to be executed simply means that the life which took visible form in me will return to its source and then, at the appointed time, will again take on this form. If my time is now at an end and I must die, then remember that it is appointed unto men once to die and after this the judgement.

Tomorrow I shall submit a petition for clemency. Perhaps the court will yet have mercy on me, and even if not, I still hope to be allowed to write to you once more. Think of me in your prayers. And now I will close, with confidence in God and in His Kingdom, and send you all my love.

ALBERT

IN OTHER LANDS
Brandenburg, 3.4.1941

To all my dear ones,
I should like to employ my last hours in writing to you once again and to ask you not to take it too hard, for it is God's will (John 19:7; Romans 8; Isaiah 59).

At 5.30 on Friday morning, April 4th, my time will have run its course and so my struggle will be at an end. My last wish is that you may live in peace and take care that none is lost (2 Timothy).

Oh my dear ones, if only I could have put on paper all the thousand things that in silent conversation I have been saying to you and am still saying. But you will find much of what I would like to say in the holy scriptures, especially the letters of the apostles, the farewell discourses of Jesus in John etc., and I hope that I shall see all of you again after my awakening.

I will close now, and you will understand why I have not written more, it would be too much. I send you my sincere greetings.

Albert

Greetings also to all the brethren and sisters and to all who think kindly of me. The grace of the Lord Jesus Christ be with you. Amen

Whatever you are, be that to the full,
Not only the bright blossom,
But also the simple leaf
Is needed for the garland.

> *Was du bist, das sei auch ganz,*
> *Nicht allein die Blüt', die lichte,*
> *Sondern auch das Blatt, das schlichte*
> *Hat Bedeutung für den Kranz.*

When West Germany emerged from the debris of the War and occupation, conscription was reintroduced to safeguard the country against attack from Russia and her communist allies. Young brethren continued to face the tribunals, although the German laws guarantee that no-one can be forced into the production or use of weapons against their conscience. To establish the sincerity of objectors, four assessors examined them, asking such questions as how the objector would react if his mother or girlfriend was attacked, sometimes subjecting the answers given to ridicule. One young brother was required to appear before the tribunal three times before being granted exemption. Those granted exemption have to undergo community service in hospitals, old peoples' homes or other suitable places.

Since the reunification of Germany, conscription has continued, although at present it is no longer necessary for most objectors to go before a tribunal. Written applications for exemption, setting out the grounds on which it is requested, are usually accepted.

Poland before the Second World War

In the early 1930s, not long before Hitler came to power, brethren and sisters from Germany held a highly successful Bible campaign in Gdansk, which at the time was known as Danzig. As a result, a small ecclesia was established in the city. Once the Nazis came to power in Germany, the city became increasingly insecure, since it was claimed to be German, although the Treaty of Versailles had given it the status of a free city at the end of the First World War. Military service became a difficult issue, since there was conscription without exemption. When the Germans invaded Poland in 1939, the city was their first objective. In the aftermath the infant ecclesia lost contact with the Brotherhood, and nothing is known at present about the fate of its members.

The Ukraine and Russia

During the period after the First World War, a young Russian Orthodox priest with an enthusiasm for Esperanto answered a tiny advertisement offering *The Declaration* in Esperanto. As a result of receiving the last remaining copy, he was baptized, followed by other members of his family and many of his flock. Driven from his parish, he moved to his wife's village, and soon a small cluster of ecclesias existed in what is now the Northern Ukraine. Brother and Sister Doubrovsky and their converts witnessed to the Truth for at least twenty-eight turbulent years.

One former Russian Orthodox church they used as the ecclesial hall in Tsepeleff was the largest Christadelphian Hall in the world. There was even a publishing house, which produced Christadelphian literature in Russian. There were also a few converts elsewhere in Russia, especially in Leningrad (now again called St. Petersburg).

Meanwhile the Communist Government of Josef Stalin launched a fierce persecution of all those held to be enemies of the State, including even some of his former comrades. In a situation where everything and everyone had to be subordinate to the needs of the state, and the atheistic Communism it preached, the ecclesias came under fierce persecution and were systematically destroyed by Stalin's agents. Virtually all the Ukrainian and Russian Christadelphians, brethren first and afterwards sisters and their young families, were forcibly transported to labour camps in Siberia or the Arctic. There they were shot or starved, or died from overwork or the cold. Only two members of these ecclesias are known to have survived the purges and the war, although visits by Brother Alan Eyre in 1992 and 1993 enabled him to track down some of their relatives (see *The Christadelphian,* 1992, page 409).

More recently, the newly baptized brethren in the independent Ukrainian and Russian states still face the problem of compulsory national service, as such service is considered a patriotic duty, and there are no liberal traditions supporting pacifism or exemption on the grounds of conscience. Similar difficulties face brethren in other former Communist states, especially where they are counted as reservists following military service in the days before their conversion. Some brethren have been imprisoned or forced to flee as a result.

A BROTHER WRITES FROM PRISON

"I'm writing exactly two weeks after arriving here. This quarantine is indeed a tough time. I have two more weeks, and then I hope my situation will change for the better. The great shame is that I am not allowed anything to read here, not even my Bible, which I had taken with me. After new year, the regime should be a bit freer. But, you know, I feel myself to be extremely strong in faith just now, in this bad situation. I remember all of you and pray strongly.

Thanks be to God, the group I will be put in after this seems to be made up of reasonable guys. They are of higher education and also there are some believers amongst them. The other three groups I could have been put into seem to be pretty low guys. But we'll see. Good news is that it was confirmed I will be given work to do relating to administration and which doesn't need use of arms.

We are allowed a very little free time to mix with the others kept here. I always talk with a guy from - - - - ; he is also a believer and it's great to be able to reason with him about everything we believe. I have to get up at 5.30 and do exercises; this is the regime here. The food isn't bad and also especially the heating is reasonable. To be honest it is better than I expected, but this must be due only to the prayers of you all.

Please thank everyone at the Bible School for their prayers for me. Another result of these prayers is that strangely they announced my quarantine has been reduced from six weeks to four weeks. It's a tragedy I won't be with my beloved brothers and sisters at the Bible School. But I will be with you in my prayers. Please relay greetings to all and tell them all that all is OK with me and they shouldn't worry about me. What I look forward to most is that after Christmas on the lighter regime I will be allowed a book, so I will be able to read the Bible! I pray every day for my brothers and sisters and especially for you: go on doing the good work of spreading the Truth, for this is the most important thing.

I am frustrated terribly that I am sitting here for a year without being able to do anything like this for the Truth. But I don't deny that God must have His plan for me. Now, about visiting me. It seems this will only be possible in six weeks after the new regime starts. But still it is unclear.

So that's all. God bless you. I only wrote to you and to my parents; it's impossible to write more. I remember our last wonderful trip! I give warm greeting to every single one. Be strong, and I too will try to set my face as a stone.

God Bless!

Your brother till the end,

V."

(From The Bible Missionary, Jan. 2001, page 5)

The Moslem World

Increasing numbers of brethren and sisters live in Moslem countries where conversion from the Moslem faith brings its own problems. There are many pressures, not only in respect of military service, but over a wide range of issues of conscience. The expansion of the Truth into these areas brings an ever greater need for courage in the face of such pressures, and for the support and constancy of those of us who are blessed with far less challenging circumstances.

11

CONCLUSIONS

*"In Flanders fields the poppies blow
Between the crosses, row on row
That mark our place; and in the sky
The larks, still bravely singing, fly,
Scarce heard among the groans below.*

*We are the Dead. Short days ago
We lived, felt dawn, saw sunset glow,
Loved and were loved, and now we lie
In Flanders fields."*

JOHN MCRAE (1915)

NO-ONE who has seen the war cemeteries of Northern France and Southern Belgium can fail to be moved by the sight of endless rows of crosses marking the graves of so many who died in the two World Wars of the last century. At Tyne Cot cemetery, close by the spot where the battle of Passchendaele was fought, there are over 20,000 graves; and the names of a huge number of those who could not be found for burial cover a great stone wall. An entry in the visitors' book on the occasion I visited identified the grave of a relative which one visitor had come to see, with the added comment, "I would rather have known him".

Such places are found in every continent—and on many former battlefields the graves of the fallen lie unmarked. How thankful we should be to be spared such carnage, and the dreadful prospect of brother encountering brother as an enemy on the field of battle. How grateful, too, that by God's grace, most of us still enjoy a large measure of freedom of conscience and at the cost of so little tribulation.

But the Christadelphian stand against military service is based on much more than abhorrence of the cruelties of war;

and it is important that we understand clearly the reasons for our conscientious objection.

FOUNDATIONS OF CONSCIENTIOUS OBJECTION

The Moral Teaching of the Lord Jesus Christ

As has already been seen in earlier chapters, the teaching of the Lord Jesus Christ plainly prohibits the use of force against even our most bitter persecutors:

> *"But I say to you who hear: Love your enemies, do good to those who hate you … and pray for those who spitefully use you."* (Luke 6:27-28)

This teaching was clearly understood by the apostles, and their converts, members of the first century ecclesias:

> *"Repay no-one evil for evil … as much as depends on you, live peaceably with all men. Beloved, do not avenge yourselves."* (Romans 12:17-19)

Not only was the teaching of Jesus clear, but the example he set of submitting to evil when he might have called on legions of angels to protect him shows unmistakably how he would have his disciples behave. At his second coming, on the other hand, he will need to use force to subdue rebellious nations who resist God's will (Revelation 17:14).

The Most High Rules in the Kingdom of Men

There is a further principle we do well to keep in mind: that God is working His purpose out in His own way in the affairs of men. However hard it may be, and however little we may understand it, we are taught by the Lord Jesus to submit to His will. It is not for us to fight to remedy the world's wrongs, nor have we any part in the politics of this world: but if it is *His* will to bring about the untold blessing of His Kingdom through the violent overthrow of His enemies, we must accept this. The evil which men do to one another would increase until the whole earth was destroyed but for the intervention of Christ at his return. Bible prophecies tell us that there will be those who are so unwilling to bow the knee to Jesus, even though they recognise him, that they will fight to resist his rule. Meantime, we have his promise that the day will come when the *"earth*

CONCLUSIONS

will be filled with the knowledge of the glory of the LORD, as the waters cover the sea" (Habakkuk 2:14), and to this we must hold fast in faith.

Another Country

Consider the following Scriptures:

> *"My kingdom is not of this world. If my kingdom were of this world, my servants would fight, so that I should not be delivered to the Jews; but now my kingdom is not from here."* (John 18:36)

> *"For many walk ... (as) enemies of the cross of Christ ... who set their mind on earthly things. For our citizenship is in heaven, from which we also eagerly wait for the Saviour, the Lord Jesus Christ."* (Philippians 3:18-20)

> *"These all died in faith ... having ... confessed that they were strangers and pilgrims on the earth. For those who say such things declare plainly that they seek a homeland ... a better ... country."* (Hebrews 11:13-16)

> *"For here we have no continuing city, but we seek the one to come."* (Hebrews 13:14)

> *"You are a chosen generation, a royal priesthood, a holy nation, his own special people ... I beg you as sojourners and pilgrims, abstain from fleshly lusts ... Therefore submit yourselves to every ordinance of man for the Lord's sake, whether to the king as supreme, or to governors ..."* (1 Peter 2:9,11-14)

> *"The day of the Lord will come as a thief in the night ... Therefore ... what manner of persons ought you to be in holy conduct and godliness, looking for and hastening the coming of the day of God? ... We, according to his promise, look for new heavens and a new earth in which righteousness dwells."* (2 Peter 3:10-13)

These quotations all make the same point: the central issue is one of loyalty. We do not fight for the kingdoms of this world because they are not our homeland. We are born into various societies and countries and do have some of the privileges and responsibilities which rest upon citizens of those countries, but this is not our pre-eminent citizenship.

THE CAPTIVE CONSCIENCE

It is our citizenship of *another country*—Christ's Kingdom—which dictates that we cannot fight in the armed forces of the present, as well as the loyalty we have to the commandments of Christ. "Our citizenship is in heaven, from which we also eagerly wait for the Saviour" (Philippians 3:20). Our stand is part of the same issue as that which dictates that we do not vote, or take part in the politics of this world. The questions of whether we should take part in civil defence, trade unions and jury service also revolve around this issue of citizenship.

Some judges who presided over Second World War tribunals understood the logic of this position. Judge Wethered was reported to have had great respect for Christadelphians, and others who believed in the Second Coming, for "none of them claimed total right of (British) citizenship". At the same time he, and many others, looked for consistency in applying this principle in the lives of those who came before them for judgement. The need for this consistency is a constant theme, to which we must now turn.

CONSISTENCY IN ALL THINGS

Time and again in these pages we have seen the importance of applying the principles of the Truth across every aspect of our lives. *The greatest argument in favour of the exemption of any Christadelphian conscientious objector is that the principles of Godly living are seen in every part of the objector's life.*

Employment

A number of the extracts in the earlier part of this work illustrate the need to ensure that we are not only regular attenders at, and supporters of, our ecclesias, but that we do not undertake employment which would compromise our position. The advice of the London Standing Committee to "Choose those occupations furthest removed from munitions work" remains very sound, and should be taken to heart by *all* brethren and sisters, even in times of peace. Similarly, any employment in which it might be necessary to use force in the course of one's duties ought to be avoided. For this reason enrolment in the Police, Special Constabulary, or other uniformed force is unacceptable to brethren and sisters in Christ. The advisability of working as a security guard must also be questioned. Indeed, any occupation in which behaviour or activities inconsistent with the Commandments of Christ is expected should be avoided.

The Law-abiding Disciple

The teaching of the Scriptures is quite clear with regard to obeying the law of the land, which we are taught to do for Christ's sake. Right from the start our brethren who made their stand against military service understood their subjection to civil authorities in other matters. The petition of the Nazarenes of 1862 stated: "We must cheerfully and heartily recognize the powers that exist ... in the capacity of civil magistrates, as God's executors for the time being, for we are explicitly commanded so to do ..."

Consequently we must beware of having a niceness of conscience in regard to fighting, but little conscience about disobeying those laws which command that we should pay taxes or keep to speed limits. The adversary is very quick to spot any inconsistency in the life of a would-be disciple, and we should exert ourselves to give him no occasion for this. Christadelphians should be model citizens with regard to the law of the land.

The Temptations of Patriotism

The issue of our citizenship raises questions of loyalty to the state or geographical area in which we live.

Naturally speaking, most of us feel some affection for the place and land in which we were brought up. Our birthplace or the place where we grew up exerts a powerful hold on us in later life, because it often represents the security of our childhood and the familiarity of surroundings which we find comforting. When the Psalmist wrote, *"How shall I sing the Lord's song in a strange land?"* he was not only mourning his separation from God's sanctuary, but also the loss of his homeland. One of the saddest comments of Scripture concerns exiles and the fate of those who were to be carried into captivity in the time of Jeremiah:

> *"Weep not for the dead ... but weep bitterly for him who goes away, for he shall return no more, nor see his native country."* (Jeremiah 22:10)

THE CAPTIVE CONSCIENCE

Whether we come from England or Scotland, Wales, Ireland, Canada, Jamaica or Kenya, few of us would welcome being banished from what we call home. Like Jeremiah, we have an attachment to our native soil which is also, in others, the basis of patriotism.

It is harder to decide when this feeling for our homeland becomes a patriotism which can compromise our position. Supporting the national football, cricket, golf, or tennis team may be relatively harmless provided such support does not get in the way of higher things, but the support given by some outside the Truth to such teams is at one end of a spectrum of patriotism which at its further extreme rejoices in military success and connives at all manner of crimes committed in war. The Falklands War in the early 1980s produced strong patriotic feelings as troop-ships set off from Portsmouth, the Belgrano was sunk, and British aircraft successfully fought against the Argentinian Air Force. Brethren and sisters in other countries, too, may have been caught up in the jingoism associated with international conflicts.

It is frightening to observe at such times how quickly moderate opinions may be swept aside in a fervour of patriotic feeling. Such feelings, and the expression of them, need to be avoided if we are to be truly those who seek another country.

Support for the Nation of Israel

We rightly feel particular interest in the land of Israel as God's Land and the Jews as God's people. We *"pray for the peace of Jerusalem"* and believe that *"they shall prosper that love thee."* As a community we have sheltered Jewish refugees, helped Jews to return to their own land, provided practical help in the building up of the Land and rejoiced in the fulfilment of prophecy. There are many who believe this to be right and proper for those who profess the Hope of Israel.

There is however a danger that we transfer our patriotism to the political State of Israel and take delight in military victories achieved by means we would deplore before a military service tribunal. For half a century, Israel has been

CONCLUSIONS

under threat from neighbouring nations, and even from terrorists within her borders. On numerous occasions Israel has successfully repulsed attacks, but more than once the Jewish state has been in grave danger. In this kind of conflict, where the difference between the aggressor and the victim seems so clear cut and the threat to Israel obvious, there is a danger that we may be provoked into making rash statements of support for political Israel. We are not political Zionists, and must accept that there are clear prophecies of disaster facing Israel associated with the return of Jesus — and that these judgements are necessary to purge from the nation the pride, the ungodliness and the confidence in their own military might which so many Israelis have.

It is a Scriptural principle that judgement begins at the House of God. The nation of Israel as it is at present is not the Kingdom of God, although the remnant of Israel will one day be at the heart of that Kingdom.

Deferred Vengeance

Sometimes brethren and sisters almost appear to relish the coming judgements of God on the earth, and may even seem to savour with enthusiasm the terrible details. Whilst it is right that we should, like Lot, be *"vexed with the filthy conversation of the wicked,"* and pray for God to intervene to bring these things to an end, bloodthirsty revelling in such an event sits uncomfortably alongside the unwillingness to fight, to which we must hold fast in the present age.

THE COST OF CONSCIENCE

We have come full circle in our survey, back to those American brethren who were prepared to be shot at their doors rather than betray their loyalty to Christ:

"We cannot and do not owe allegiance to any other."

And through the centuries, from those who faced lions and gladiators in the Roman amphitheatres, through scattered pockets of true belief in the Middle Ages and the better documented stand of the Brethren in Christ of the sixteenth century, to the young brethren who faced tribunals in the past hundred years, we have seen a consistent position of conscientious objection to military service.

THE CAPTIVE CONSCIENCE

But for some, mostly out of our view and in countries other than our own, the cost of conscience has been high. A brother shot at dawn; whole ecclesias apparently destroyed in Russia and Poland; brethren imprisoned, suffering mistreatment and contempt; and nearer at hand, lives uprooted by command of tribunals; careers disrupted by company attitudes to objectors; and families separated from those they loved.

And sometimes we may have been tempted to avoid paying the price, and compromised in ways which look shameful beside such sacrifices; and perhaps we have not always been clear about the principles of our stand. For some few, the pressures have been too great, and they have left the Christadelphian community rather than endure them.

How can we be ready?

"This know also," writes the Apostle Paul to Timothy and to us, *"that in the last days perilous times shall come"* (2 Timothy 3:1, AV).

We are sometimes curiously myopic in our use of these words, happy to point out to the unbeliever that they foretell terrible times to come before the return of Christ, but strangely reluctant to recognise that in the final days of this world we may ourselves once more be called upon to make a stand for our faith. We have no way of knowing exactly what form this may take or what sacrifices it may demand. But now is the time for us to prepare to face whatever may come according to His will. And we have this advice from the Apostle Paul, as he waited in the condemned cell to pay the full price of his commitment to his Lord:

"Preach the word! Be ready in season and out of season."

In other words, we must not be ashamed of the Gospel of Christ. Our neighbours will not be impressed if the first time they know of our faith is when we ask to be excused military service!

"Continue in the things you have learned and been assured of", for there is no substitute for daily reading and discussion of the Scriptures, through which we gain a clear understanding of the principles of our stand.

CONCLUSIONS

"Keep the faith" and live it daily, for only by taking up the cross and following Jesus with a full heart can we live consistent lives which honour God.

"Love his appearing", for that is what helped those who suffered and died in the past to know that it was all worthwhile.

THE PRIVILEGE OF FAITH

Many of those who contributed material to this book spoke of the privilege of faithful witness to the truth, referring time and time again to the sense of fellowship bred by hardship and persecution. Many of those who came in contact with them as potential adversaries in courtrooms and guard-houses were moved to envy, at least a little, a faith which had so much steadfastness to serve the Lord Christ, and so much conviction of a better world which would come, not by human endeavour, but by the coming of Jesus as Saviour and King. And that faith transcends frontiers and colour and language and nationality. For the Apostle Paul says:

"There is neither Greek nor Jew, circumcised nor uncircumcised, barbarian, Scythian, slave nor free, but Christ is all and in all." (Colossians 3:11)

To Christ we live and for him, if needs be, we ought even to be ready to face death, for he himself has died to give us life and hope and glory:

"Therefore let us go forth to him, outside the camp, bearing his reproach. For here we have no continuing city, but we seek the one to come." (Hebrews 13:13-14)

For it is this Lord, this Faith, this City to which our consciences must be captive—now and ever. Amen.

BIBLIOGRAPHY

The works referred to have been arranged chronologically with regard to the date of publication or the period to which they refer. In addition to books and pamphlets, reference was made to letters and circulars to ecclesias, particularly those from the UK Military Service Committee. ND: date of publication unknown; NP: no place of publication indicated; MS: an unpublished manuscript.

Books and Pamphlets by Christadelphian Authors
1873—1930

Roberts, Robert, *Dr. Thomas: His Life and Work* (Birmingham, 1873).
> This biography covers the period of the American Civil War and gives an account of the original stand made against fighting.

Dr. Thomas on Conscription during the American Civil War (Bristol, c. 1900).
> Reprints from answers to correspondents, 1859—1865.

Walker, C. C., *Christ and War* (Birmingham, 1900).
> "A Lecture by the Editor of *The Christadelphian*."

Military Service Committee, *Evidence (extending over half a century) that Conscientious Objection to Military Service and the Bearing of Arms is a Denominational Characteristic of the Christadelphian Body of Believers, 1860—1915* (London, 1915; later editions published in Birmingham).
> Brethren and sisters enclosed this booklet with their applications for exemption.

Walker, Frank (ed.), *The Young Worker's Advocate and Mutual Magazine*.
> Issues for March, May, June, July and August 1915, August 1916 and January 1917, contain articles and news about World War I and the position of young brethren.

Collyer, Islip, *The Curse of War* (London, 1916).

Denney, G. H. and Newnham, F. G. (eds.), *Christadelphian Year Book 1916* (Bristol, 1916).
> Contains interesting insights into the circumstances of ecclesias in the First World War, with topical cartoons of the time.

Jannaway, Frank G., *Without the Camp* (London, 1917).
> Brother Frank Jannaway's account of how Christadelphians obtained exemption from military service in World War I.

The London Standing Committee, *Christadelphians and Military Service* (London, 1918).
> Covers much of the same ground as *Without the Camp*.

Jannaway, Frank G., *Lest We Forget* (London, 1923).
> A small book produced during the controversy of the time about membership of the Royal Army Medical Corps and the Police.

Jannaway, Frank G., *Christadelphians during the Great War* (London, 1929).
> An abbreviated account of the circumstances that led to Christadelphian exemption in World War I (produced when *Without the Camp* was out of print).

1930—1957

Jannaway, Frank G., *Christadelphians and Military Service* (NP, 1932).
> A curious booklet "forming Appendix VII of *Without the Camp*".

Statement by the Christadelphian Military Service Committee (NP, 1936).
> A circular sent to all ecclesias at the time when German revival under Hitler began to threaten renewed war.

Collyer, Islip, *A Second Letter to Young Christadelphians* (Kenilworth, 1937).

Collyer, Islip, *A Third Letter to Young Christadelphians* (Coventry, 1939).
> Two letters encouraging young people to remain steadfast; the *Third Letter* has particular reference to military service.

"Birmingham Holds First Militia Act Tribunal"—Report in the *Birmingham Evening Despatch*, July 27, 1939.
> One of many newspaper cuttings reviewed during the preparation of this book.

BIBLIOGRAPHY

The Christadelphian Civil Defence Committee, *Our Citizenship* (NP, January 1942).
> A pamphlet by a group of brethren arguing "The Bible case against participation by Christadelphians in Civil Defence".

The Christadelphian Civil Defence Committee, *Freedom or Bondage* (NP, January 1942).
> A pamphlet presenting "The answer to the case of the Military Service Committee for participation in Civil Defence".

A Statement Setting Forth the Grounds for Christadelphian Scriptural Objection to Service in Civil Defence Forces (National Service Acts 1941) (NP, February 1942).
> A circular published by a group of brethren opposed to Christadelphians participating in Civil Defence.

Collyer, Islip, *A Solemn Warning to Christadelphians* (NP, March 1942).
> A leaflet opposing the conclusions put forward in *Our Citizenship* and *Freedom or Bondage*.

Unpublished papers of Brother Gordon Ramsden detailing cases of Suffolk Street brethren (1945–1957, MS).

Norris, J. B., *The Christian and War* (Birmingham, 1954).
> An invaluable scriptural and historical study, with details of the position of believers in the early centuries.

1957–Present

Smalley, H. F. and Jennings, L. C., *Christ and War; Christian and State* (Birmingham, ND).
> A two-part pamphlet published by the Christadelphian Advisory Committee, Suffolk Street.

Bilton, Percy, *". . must not FIGHT"* (London, 1964).
> A pamphlet explaining the Christian's objections to fighting.

Pearce, Graham, *Are we ready for another Time of Testing?* (Crick, 1971).
> A pamphlet arguing for separation, and for seeking unconditional exemption in a time of national emergency.

Eyre, Alan, *The Protesters* (Birmingham, 1975; 1985).

Eyre, Alan, *Brethren in Christ* (S. Australia, 1982).
> Two books exploring the history of groups down the ages who sought to maintain the principles of First Century Christianity.

THE CAPTIVE CONSCIENCE

Morris, J. H., *The Peace Movements: Where does the Disciple Stand?* (Birmingham, 1984).

Barker, Jayne, *The Christadelphians and World War I* (Manchester Polytechnic Dissertation, 1990).

Reekie, Peter, *Exemption* (London, March 1993).
> A digest of Brother Viner Hall's writings on conscientious objection to military service during World War I and after.

Richardson, Len, *Sixty Years a Christadelphian* (NP, 1993).
> Includes a personal account of the experiences of a conscientious objector in World War II.

Hemingray, Peter, *Dr. Thomas: His Faith and His Friends* (Michigan, USA, MS, to be published).
> The results of recent research, including chapters on Brother Thomas's initiatives during the American Civil War.

Material relating to other Countries

Canadian Christadelphian Standing Committee, *A Summary of the Work of the Christadelphian Standing Committee, 1917–1919* (Toronto, 1919, reprinted 1970).

Weir, W., *A Summary Report of the Work of the Christadelphian Standing Committee 1920–1945* (Canada, c. 1970).

Pook, K. M., *The Christian's Relations with the State* (Canada, ND; also printed by C. G. Ramsden, London).
> The disciple's heavenly and earthly citizenship contrasted.

Correspondence relating to the Australian Christadelphian Ecclesias' Request for Exemption from Military Service, 1939–41 (Unpublished papers).

Christadelphian Service Committee, *The Historic Position of the Christadelphians as Religious Conscientious Objectors* (1952).
> Leaflet containing extracts from US Government and other publications for use by brethren in North America.

Canadian Christadelphian Service Committee, *The Christadelphian Position with respect to Military Service* (Ontario, 1965).

Australian Central Standing Committee, *Politics, Law Enforcement and Brotherhood in Christ* (Sydney, 1968).

BIBLIOGRAPHY

Evans, E. R., *Test Case for Canada '3314545'* (Canada, 1972).
> The experiences of Brother John Evans in World War I.

Cowie, J. A., *Conscientious Objection to Military Service* (Queensland, ND).
> A manual designed to assist Australian young people in the 1970s facing the prospect of national service call-up.

Conscientious Objection: The Christadelphian's Relation with the State (S. Australia, 1981).

Circular Letters of the Canadian Standing Committee (1983; 1987).

Statement by the South African Military Service Committee to the Authorities (Unpublished, 1984).

Report on the Proceedings of the Meeting of the Board for Religious Objection held in Bloemfontein, South Africa (March 15, 1984).
> The history of conscientious objection in South Africa.

Oosthuizen, Anthony J., "Religious Objection to Military Service—A Historical Perspective", in *Journal of the University of Durban-Westville,* New Series 3 (1986).
> Contains reference to the Christadelphian position.

Newsletters of the South African Military Service Committee (from No.1, 1986).

Unpublished letter relating to National Service in Guyana (1986).

Payne, Deborah and Beer, Suzanne, *In Defence of our Conscience* (S. Australia, 1987).
> A history of conscientious objection among the New Zealand ecclesias compiled for the Wellington Ecclesia.

Sommerville, D., *Civilian Public Service Memo* (Ohio, 1988).
> Pamphlet recounting Brother David Sommerville's experiences as a CO in a Civilian Public Service Camp, 1941-1945.

Evans, E. R., *"Ye are strangers and sojourners with me"* (Canada, 1990).
> An interesting look at Christadelphian teaching on relationships with the State.

Waddoup, L. Roy, *The Truth in Germany* (Weston-super-Mare, 1995).
> History of German Christadelphians, particularly the early years, and including reference to Brother Albert Merz.

Non-Christadelphian Works

Russell, Bertrand, *Power: A New Social Analysis* (1940).
> Has this comment on Christadelphians: "Christianity was, in its earliest days, entirely unpolitical. The best representatives of the primitive tradition in our time are the Christadelphians, who believe the end of the world to be imminent, and refuse to have any part or lot in secular affairs."

Field, G. C., *Pacifism and Conscientious Objection* (1945).
> This author makes a very similar comment to the above.

Central Board for Conscientious Objectors, *Conscientious Objectors: Their Position in 1953*.
> A report of a debate in the House of Commons in July 1953.

Barker, Rachel, *Conscience, Government and War* (1982).
> A very full and well-researched account of the mechanisms and attitudes of Second World War tribunals and their impact on conscientious objectors, based on the original tribunal records, newspaper accounts of the time and other primary sources. Contains numerous references to Christadelphians.

Casey, Michael W., *From the Nazarenes to the Christadelphians: The Story of Pacifism in the Christadelphians* (MS, to be published in the USA).

CMPA and Military Service Committee Pamphlets

Norris, A. D., *The Gospel and Politics* (1970).

Norris, A. D., *The Gospel and Strife* (1981).

Tennant, Harry, *Christ and Protest: The Bible Answer to Revolution and Human Rights* (1986).

Twelves, H. A., *The Disciple and Jury Service* (1984).

Butler, C. T., *The Disciple of Christ and Trade Unions* (1990).

Christadelphian Bible Mission Pamphlets

Watkins, Peter, *War and Politics: The Christian's Duty* (1976).

East, Arthur, *War, Aggression and the Christian Life* (2001).

INDEX

AIR RAIDS 79
Air Raid Patrols (ARP) 63,72
Alternative service
   3,90,102-104
Ambassador of the Coming
  Age 6,7,23
Ambulance Work 47,63,75
American Civil War 1-8,100
Antipas Association of
  Christadelphians 5,6
Apostolic Advocate 7
Applications for Exemption
   42,43,58,64-66
Augustine 12,13
Australia 27,92-95

BIBLE reading 26,112,120
Biddle, John 21
Birmingham 49
Birmingham (Central)
  Fellowship 83,90
Birmingham (Suffolk St.)
  Fellowship 59,83,90
Birmingham Temperance
  Hall Ecclesia 36,51
Boer War 26,84,95
Bournemouth 40
Boys and Girls, Registration
  Order 76
Brethren in Christ 6-8,19,21
Bristol 39

CADET Corps 76,84,104

Call-up Papers 41
Canada 88-92
Carter, Bro. John 57,83,86,91
Casualties 79
Central Benevolent Fund 86
Central Bureau of
  Conscientious Objectors 74
Certificate of Exemption
   34,44,45,66
Certificate identifying
  Christadelphians (USA) 4-6
Certificate of Membership 59
Chamberlain, Neville 54
Charlemagne 15
Children, Registration 76
Christadelphian, The
  3,23,26,27,31,34,60,77,111
Christadelphian Isolation
  League 77
Christadelphian Youth
  Circles, Origins of 76
Christadelphians, Origin of
  Name 4-8
Christian and War, The 14
"Christians" in Roman Army
   11
Church Attitudes 32
—Catholic Church 15
—Church of England 32
Citizenship 67,73,115
City of God, The 12
Civil Defence 72-74,82,116

THE CAPTIVE CONSCIENCE

Cold War 88,103
Comments on Christadelphians (see Tribunals)
Conscientious Objection
v,vii,2,56,104
Conscientious Objectors in the Armed Forces 10,25,70
Conscription vii
–American Civil War 1-8,100
–Australia 92-95
–Canada 88-92
–Europe in the Late 19th Century 23,24
–Germany 105-109
–New Zealand 84-88
–Roman Empire 10
–Sisters 74-76
–South Africa 95-99
–South African (Boer) War 26,84,95
–United States of America 100-104
–World War I in Britain 32
–World War II in Britain 55
Consistency, Importance of 57,66,102,116,117,119,121
Courts Martial 40,70,87,89,102
Coventry 49,79
Criticism, Mockery and Taunting of COs 45,78,87,88,102
Crusades 16
CYC Membership 76

DETENTION (see also Imprisonment) 97
Diocletian 12

Disfellowshipping of Brethren joining Military Forces 11,21,66
Dr. Thomas: His Life and Work 8
Draft, in USA 2,100,103

EASTERN Europe 20,41,110-112
Ecclesial Registers, Importance of 35,36,83
El Salvador 105
Employment (see Occupations)
English Civil War 21
Eusebius 12
Evans, Bro. John 89,90
Evidence booklet 59,81
Execution for Conscientious Objection 12,106-109
Exemption on Religious Grounds 2,45
–Absolute/Unconditional 34,37,58,59,64-66,100
–Conditional 37,44,58,59,109
–From Combatant Service 37,88,94
Exemption Committee (USA) 102

FAITH 50,121
Falklands War vii,118
Farming (see Land Work)
Fascism 52,90
Federal Bureau of Investigation 100
Fellowship, Strengthened 77,121
Fine or Payment to avoid Conscription 2,3,7
Fire Service 91
Firefighting 73,103

INDEX

Firewatching	73-75
First Century Believers	9,114
First World War (see World War I)	
Forestry	47,48,85,91
French Revolution	24
GDANSK	110
Germany	105-110
Gladstone, William	25
God, Commitment to	64,108
Great War (see World War I)	
Grebel, Conrad	19
Gulf War	vii
Guyana	104
HALL, Bro. Viner	36,73
Herald of the Kingdom and Age to Come	1
Hippolytus	11
Hitler, Adolf	52,106
Holy Roman Emperor	15
"Holy" War	16
Home Guard	71
Hospital Work	3,47,69,75,103,109
Hypocrisy	13,116-119
IMPRISONMENT of Objectors (see also Detention)	40,45,70,74,81,87,88,100,106,111
Industrial Conscription	74
Interviewing of Candidates for Baptism	35,36,66
Invasion Plans	71
Israel, Support for	118
JAMAICA	105
Jannaway, Bro. Frank	41-50
Jehovah's Witnesses	81,104
Jerusalem	10,16
Jesus Christ	
–Allegiance to	3
–Commandments of	9,14,21,26,114,115
–Second Coming	v,25,28,116,121
Jewish Christians	10
Jewish Revolt, AD 70	10
Jingoism	118
Josephus	10
Judgements of God	119
Jury Service	116
"Just" War	12,13,32,53
KAISER, Bro. Colin	97
Kingdom of God	22,25,114,119
Kitchener Poster	30,101
Knighthood	16
Korean War	95
LAND Work	47,48,68,69
Law, Importance of Obeying	28,34,40,65,117
Lightstand magazine	97
Living the Truth, Importance of	64,116-121
London Standing Committee	34-53
Lunenburg County (VA)	7
Luther, Martin	18
MAXIMILIAN	12
Membership Certificates	59
Mennonites	104
Merz, Bro. Albert	106-109
Middle Ages	15-17,119
Military Affairs Committee (USA)	103
Military Oath	36
Military Service Acts	33,59

Military Service Committee vi,vii,53,55,82
Mines, Work in 69,91
Ministers of the Gospel, Exemption for 4
Mitchell, Bro. Fred 61,82,83
Mock Tribunals 67
Moslem world 112
Munitions Work 49,51,53,94,95
Müntzer, Thomas 19

NAPOLEONIC WARS 24
National Fire Service 73,75
National Registration Act 1915 32,36
National Service Act 1941 72
National Service (post-war) 80
National Youth Service (Jamaica) 105
Nationalism v,41
Nazarenes, The 3,6-8,117
New York 5
New Zealand 27,84-88
Non-Combatant Service 21,38,40,59,85,96,100,103
Non-Conformists 17

OATHS 11,36,39,75,94
Occupations
–Advice on 53,116
–Approved 47
–Loss of Occupation 48-50,69,78,81
–Reserved 37,46,58
Ogle County (IL) 4
Origen 11

PACIFISM 17,52,58,66
Patriotism 29,32,66,73,117

Paul, Words on Not Resisting Evil 114,115,120
Peace Movements 52
–Peace Pledge Union 52
"Peace of God" 15,17
Peace Society 7
Peasants' War 18,19
Persecution (see also Suffering for Conscience Sake) 119,121
Personal Conviction, Importance of 57,61,116
Peter
–Words on Not Resisting Evil 99,115
–Takes Sword 40
Petitions
–1878 25
–1903 27
–1914 28
–Australian 93-95
–Jersey City 100
–Lincoln 28
–Nazarenes 3,8
–New Zealand 84
–US Congress 6
Poland 20,110
Police 73,82,116
Politics 63,114,116
"Powers that be" 3,5
Prayer 33,46,58,68,112
Preparing for Tribunals 58-68
Prison (see Imprisonment and Detention)
Privilege of Witnessing 121
Protestants 18-22
Providential Care 78,79

QUAKERS 87,104

INDEX

Questions asked by
  Tribunals   61-64
RAILWAYS, Work on 47,48,64
Rally for Christadelphian
  Objectors   59-61
Ramsden, Bro. Gordon 42,82
Recruitment   3,30,55,101
Red Cross   47,63,88,91
Reformation   17,18,21
Register of bona fide
  Christadelphians   44,59,60
Registers, Ecclesial 35,36,83
Reserved Occupations
                      37,46,58
Reservists   111
Responsibility to God 64,107
Responsibility to the State 65
Richmond (VA)   7
Roberts, Bro. Robert   23
Roman Catholic Church
                         13-17
Roman Empire   9-14,119
Rowntree, Arnold   28
Royal Army Medical Corps
                      37,38,63
Royal Association of
  Believers   6
Rugby   39
Russell, Bertrand   128
Russia and the Ukraine
                     110-112

SARGENT, Bro. L. G.   77
Sattler, Michael   19
Scriptural Basis of
  Conscientious Objection
        25,90,93,114,115
Second Coming, Belief in
        v,25,28,116,121
Second World War (see World
  War II)

Security Guards   117
Sisters and Conscription 74-76
Six-Day War   83
South Africa   95-99
South African (Boer) War
                    26,84,95
Spanish Civil War   53,72
Special Constabulary 64,116
Standby Draft   103
State, Attitude to   65
Statement of Faith   44,93
Stuttgart   105,106
Suffering for Conscience
  Sake   v,18-22,45,78,
       87,92,106-109,120
Sunday Work   36,68
TERTULLIAN   11
Test Case of 1916   41-44
Thirty Years' War   18
Thomas, Bro. John   1-8,23
Thomasites   6,8
Trade Unions   63,116
Tribunals   37-44,56-68,109
–Advisory   70
–Area Appeals   38
–Central Appeal   38,42-44
–Comments of Judges
               61,66,67,116
–Local   37
"Truce of God"   17
Turkish Empire   24
Twofold Catechism, The   21
UKRAINE   110
United States of America
                      100-104
–American Civil War 1-8,100
–Militia Law   3
–Selective Service Act   100
–World War I   100-102
–World War II   103,104

VAUDOIS	17
Vietnam War	95,103
Voting	52,116
WALDENSES	17
Walker, Bro. C.C.	27,49
War in God's Purpose	98,99,114
War Loans	63
Withdrawal for Attitude on Military Service	31,66,105
Without the Camp	50
Wolzogen, Johann	20,21
Women, Compulsory Registration	75
Work of National Importance	37,44,46-48,58,68
World War I	29-51,84,88-90,100-102,105
World War II	54-79,85-88,90-96,103,104,106-109
Wycliffe, John	17
YAHWEH ELOHIM (pamphlet)	5
Young People, Registration	76
Young Worker's Advocate and Mutual Magazine	30,39,49
Youth Circles	76
ZIONISM	119